WOMAN TO WOMAN
BEYOND STEREOTYPES AND STATUS

General Editor
LYMAN COLEMAN

Managing Editor
DENISE BELTZNER

Assistant Editors
DOUGLAS LABUDDE
KEITH MADSEN
STEPHEN SHEELY

Cover Art
CHRISTOPHER WERNER

Cover Design
ERIKA TIEPEL

Layout Production
FRONTLINE GROUP
MAURICE LYDICK

Seven Issues Women Need to Talk About

SESSION	ENTRY LEVEL	ADVANCED LEVEL
1 ORIENTATION	A Virtuous Woman: Proverbs 31:10–31	
2 PURSUING BALANCE	Queen of Sheba: 1 Kings 10:1–10, 13	Lydia: Acts 16:11–15
3 PURUSING WHOLENESS	Bathsheba: 2 Samuel 11:1–5, 14–17, 26–27	Woman With the Issue of Blood: Luke 8:42b–48
4 PURSUING HEALTHY RELATIONSHIPS	Ruth and Naomi: Ruth 1:3–18	Elizabeth: selections from Luke 1
5 PURSUING A LIFE OF SERVICE	A Shunammite Woman: 2 Kings 4:8–17	Dorcas: Acts 9:36–42
6 PURSUING A LIFE OF FAITH	Sarah: Genesis 18:1–2, 9–15; 21:1–7	Mary, Mother of Jesus: John 2:1–11
7 PURSUING OUR POTENTIAL	Deborah: Judges 4:1–16	Priscilla: Acts 18:18–28

Serendipity House / Box 1012 / Littleton, CO 80160   1-800-525-9563

ACKNOWLEDGMENTS

To Zondervan Bible Publishers
for permission to use
the NIV text,
The Holy Bible, New International Bible Society.
© 1973, 1978, 1984 by International Bible Society.
Used by permission of Zondervan Bible Publishers

Instructions for Group Leader

PURPOSE:

What is this course all about? This course allows you to deal with women's issues in a supportive group relationship.

SEEKERS/ STRUGGLERS:

Who is this course designed for? Two kinds of people:(a) Seekers who do not know where they are with God but are open to finding out, and (b) Strugglers who are committed to Jesus Christ, but want to grow in their faith.

NEW PEOPLE:

Does this mean I can invite my non-church friends? Absolutely. In fact, this would be a good place for people on their way back to God to start.

STUDY:

What are we going to study? Seven issues women need to talk about (see inside front cover), and Biblical strategies for dealing with them.

FIRST SESSION:

What do we do at the meetings? In the first session, you get acquainted and decide on the Ground Rules for your group. In sessions two through seven, you have two Options for Bible study.

TWO OPTIONS:

What are the two options? OPTION ONE—This study is best for newly-formed groups or groups that are unfamiliar with small group Bible study. This option primarily contains multiple-choice questions, with no "right or wrong" answers.

OPTION TWO—This study is best for groups who have had previous small group Bible studies and want to dig deeper into the Scriptures. Option Two questions are deeper—and the Scripture is a teaching passage.

CHOOSING AN OPTION:

Which option of Bible study do you recommend? The OPTION ONE study is best for newly-formed groups, groups that are unfamiliar with small group Bible study, or groups that are only meeting for an hour. The OPTION TWO study is best for deeper Bible study groups, or groups which meet for more than an hour.

CHOOSING BOTH OPTIONS:	**Can we choose both options?** If your group meets for 90 to 120 minutes, you can choose to do both studies at the same time. Or you can spend two weeks on a unit—OPTION ONE the first week and OPTION TWO the next. Or you can do one of the options in the meeting and the other option for homework.
SMALL GROUP:	**What's different about this course?** It is written for a small group to do together.
GROUP BUILDING:	**What is the purpose behind your approach to Bible study?** To give everyone a chance to share their own "spiritual story," and to bond as a group. This is often referred to as "koinonia."
KOINONIA:	**What is koinonia and why is it a part of these studies?** Koinonia means "fellowship." It is an important part of these sessions, because as a group gets to know one another, they are more willing to share their needs and care for one another.
BIBLE KNOWLEDGE:	**What if I don't know much about the Bible?** No problem. Option One is based on a Bible story that stands on its own—to discuss as though you were hearing it for the first time. Option Two comes with Comments—to keep you up to speed.
COMMENTS:	**What is the purpose of the Comments in the studies?** To help you understand the context of the Bible passage.
LEADERSHIP:	**Who leads the meetings?** Ideally, there should be three people: (a) trained leader, (b) apprentice or co-leader, and (c) host. Having an apprentice-in-training in the group, you have a built-in system for multiplying the group if it gets too large. In fact, this is one of the goals of the group—to give "birth" to a new group in time.

Beginning a Small Group

1. AGENDA: There are three parts to every group meeting.

GATHERING	BIBLE STUDY	CARING TIME
15 min.	30 min.	15–45 min.
Purpose:	Purpose:	Purpose:
To break the ice	To share your spiritual journey	To share prayer requests

2. FEARLESS FOURSOME: If you have more than seven in your group at any time, call the option play when the time comes for Bible study, and subdivide into groups of 4 for greater participation. (In 4's, everyone will share and you can finish the Bible study in 30 minutes). Then regather the group for the CARING TIME.

GATHERING	BIBLE STUDY	CARING TIME
All Together	Groups of 4	Back Together

3. EMPTY CHAIR: Pull up an empty chair during the CARING TIME at the close and ask God to fill this chair each week. Remember, by breaking into groups of four for the Bible study time, you can grow numerically without feeling "too big" as a group.

The Group Leader needs an apprentice-in-training at all times so that the apprentice can start a new "cell" when the group size is 12 or more.

SESSION 1
Orientation

PURPOSE To get acquainted, to share your expectations, and to decide on the ground rules for your group.

AGENDA   **Gathering**   **Bible Study**   **Caring Time**

OPEN   **GATHERING / 15 Minutes / All Together**
Leader: The purpose of the Gathering time is to break the ice. Read the instructions for Step One and go first. Then read the Introduction (Step Two) and the instructions for the Bible Study.

Step One: LET ME TELL YOU ABOUT MY DAY. What was your day like today? Or your week? Month? Year? Choose one of the items below to help you describe your day to the group. Feel free to elaborate, but allow enough time for each group member to share. "My day was like ..."

❏ a Greek tragedy   ❏ a soap opera
❏ a fairy tale   ❏ the late night news
❏ a Sharon Stone movie   ❏ a Bible epic
❏ a boring lecture   ❏ a professional tennis match
❏ a fireworks display   ❏ a rainy spring day
❏ a Calgon bath commercial
❏ an episode of The Three Stooges

INTRODUCTION **Step Two: WELCOME.** Welcome to this course on issues women need to talk about. In this session, we will get an overview of what we will study for these seven sessions, as well as become acquainted, and decide on the ground rules for this group.

Today's woman has numerous demands placed on her and on her time. So we may think the last thing we have time for is a Bible Study on women. Perhaps it will be the best thing we can do. Often, in the hustle and bustle of everyday life, we do not take (or have) the time to look at the bigger picture of our lives.

There is no doubt the role of women has changed dramatically over the past few decades. Women are entering the work force in record numbers. We are trying to juggle all of our increased responsibilities. We are being more intentional about realizing our full potential. And our full potential includes caring for ourselves, for our family and friends, and for others. We have homes, careers, relationships, and hopefully a personal life.

One of the advertisements in the 1970s stressed that "we have come a long way baby," and we have. Or have we? We feel that since the beginning of the Women's Movement so much has changed. But we can't identify with some of those changes. Plus there have been many misconceptions about God's view of women over the centuries. In our first session together, we will look at the famous passage of the virtuous woman taken from the book of Proverbs. As we study this passage, we will see that this virtuous woman sounds like today's liberated woman!

And in the subsequent sessions, we will look at some of the women of the Bible and glean bits of insight and wisdom from their lives. This is a book of pursuits. We will look at women who pursued balance (a career and a personal life), wholeness (physical and emotional), relationships, a life of service, a life of faith, and their full potential.

THREE PARTS TO A SESSION

Every session has three parts: (1) **Gathering**—to break the ice and introduce the topic, (2) **Bible Study**—to share your own study through a passage of Scripture, and (3) **Caring Time**—to decide what action you need to take in this area of your life and to support one another in this action. Following the Bible Study is a section entitled Comment. It contains a few words about the woman we studied in the Bible Study. The two resources used (apart from the Bible) are *The New Bible Dictionary* (edited by J.D. Douglas) and *All of the Women of the Bible* by Edith Deen.

In this course, the Bible Study approach is a little unique with a different focus. Usually, the content of the passage is the focus of the Bible Study. In this course, the focus will be on telling your "story," using the passage as a springboard. In addition, this book is set up a bit differently than the other studies in this series. The first option will be from an Old Testament passage and the second option will be a New Testament passage.

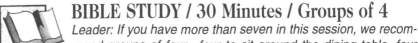

BIBLE STUDY / 30 Minutes / Groups of 4

Leader: If you have more than seven in this session, we recommend groups of four—four to sit around the dining table, four around the kitchen table, and four around a folding table. Ask one person in each foursome to be the Convener and to complete the Bible Study in the time allowed. Then regather for the Caring Time, allowing 20 minutes.

STUDY Read the following Scripture, which is from Proverbs 31. This passage is often called the "virtuous woman chapter." It is King Lemuel's (or perhaps his mother's—see verse 1) attempt to show the characteristics of a virtuous woman, not just a virtuous wife. These verses form an acrostic; that is, each verse begins with the next letter of the Hebrew alphabet. In each foursome, ask someone to be the Convener. Go around on the first question. Then go around on the next question, working through the questionnaire. After 30 minutes, the leader will call time and ask you to regather for the Caring Time.

> *[10]A wife of noble character who can find?*
>   *She is worth far more than rubies.*
> *[11]Her husband has full confidence in her*
>   *and lacks nothing of value.*
> *[12]She brings him good, not harm,*
>   *all the days of her life.*
> *[13]She selects wool and flax*
>   *and works with eager hands.*
> *[14]She is like the merchant ships,*
>   *bringing her food from afar.*
> *[15]She gets up while it is still dark;*
>   *she provides food for her family*
>   *and portions for her servant girls.*
> *[16]She considers a field and buys it;*
>   *out of her earnings she plants a vineyard.*
> *[17]She sets about her work vigorously;*
>   *her arms are strong for her tasks.*
> *[18]She sees that her trading is profitable,*
>   *and her lamp does not go out at night.*
> *[19]In her hand she holds the distaff*
>   *and grasps the spindle with her fingers.*
> *[20]She opens her arms to the poor*
>   *and extends her hands to the needy.*
> *[21]When it snows, she has no fear for her household;*
>   *for all of them are clothed in scarlet.*
> *[22]She makes coverings for her bed;*
>   *she is clothed in fine linen and purple.*
> *[23]Her husband is respected at the city gate,*
>   *where he takes his seat among the elders of the land.*
> *[24]She makes linen garments and sells them,*
>   *and supplies the merchants with sashes.*
> *[25]She is clothed with strength and dignity;*
>   *she can laugh at the days to come.*
> *[26]She speaks with wisdom,*
>   *and faithful instruction is on her tongue.*
> *[27]She watches over the affairs of her household*
>   *and does not eat the bread of idleness.*
> *[28]Her children arise and call her blessed;*
>   *her husband also, and he praises her:*

[29]*"Many women do noble things,*
but you surpass them all."
[30]*Charm is deceptive, and beauty is fleeting;*
but a woman who fears the LORD is to be praised.
[31]*Give her the reward she has earned,*
and let her works bring her praise at the city gate.

Proverbs 31:10–31, NIV

1. What is your initial reaction to King Lemuel's words about a virtuous woman?
   - ❏ She is the superwoman of the '90s.
   - ❏ She reminds me of myself.
   - ❏ She must be very tired!
   - ❏ Anything I can do, she can do better.
   - ❏ Attaining the status of a virtuous woman is impossible.

2. From this passage of Scripture, how would the ideal woman define her "place"?
   - ❏ the house, making meals and clothes
   - ❏ the House and Senate, making major decisions
   - ❏ the market, buying groceries and cloth
   - ❏ the Market (Wall Street), wheeling and dealing
   - ❏ the marketplace, being an entrepreneur

3. Of all the "things" this woman manages, which do you feel is the most important? Why?
   - ❏ the household
   - ❏ the family
   - ❏ property
   - ❏ her personal life
   - ❏ her business partnership
   - ❏ the domestic help
   - ❏ money
   - ❏ other: _____

4. How can anyone become like this woman?
   - ❏ She isn't a real person—only a symbol for a spiritual quality.
   - ❏ She is a real woman, but no one I've ever known.
   - ❏ She is an ideal woman we should aspire to emulate.
   - ❏ We can be like her with a little time management help.
   - ❏ We can be like her if we have domestic help.
   - ❏ We can't be like her—she is the culmination of everything good in women, and we can't reach that level of perfection.

5. Who does the woman in this passage most remind you of?
   - ❏ my mother
   - ❏ myself now
   - ❏ a woman in the neighborhood (or church) I grew up in as a child
   - ❏ one of my grandmothers
   - ❏ no woman I have ever met

6. This passage says of this woman, "Her children arise and call her blessed." What was particularly "blessed" about your mother when you were a child?
   - ❏ her devotion to her husband
   - ❏ her business or economic insight
   - ❏ the sacrifices she made for the family
   - ❏ her concern for the poor and oppressed
   - ❏ her ability to provide for her family
   - ❏ her inner strength and dignity
   - ❏ her ability to laugh in the face of adversity
   - ❏ her wisdom
   - ❏ her hard work
   - ❏ her belief in God
   - ❏ other: _____

7. Which of the following women do you consider a role model for you (or for your daughters)?
   - ❏ Eleanor Roosevelt
   - ❏ Margaret Thatcher
   - ❏ Hillary Rodham Clinton
   - ❏ Tipper Gore
   - ❏ Oprah Winfrey
   - ❏ Mary Lou Retton
   - ❏ Mother Teresa
   - ❏ Ruth Bell Graham
   - ❏ Joni Eareckson Tada
   - ❏ Rosalyn Carter
   - ❏ Florence Griffith-Joyner
   - ❏ other: _____

8. Name two features of the woman you chose in question #7 that you admire.

9. The woman in this passage excelled in many areas. Choose an area you would like to focus on for yourself:
   - ❏ devotion to my husband or significant other
   - ❏ business or economic acumen
   - ❏ willingness to sacrifice for the people I care about
   - ❏ showing concern for the poor and oppressed
   - ❏ being a good provider
   - ❏ having inner strength and dignity
   - ❏ having an ability to laugh in the face of adversity
   - ❏ showing wisdom
   - ❏ being a hard worker
   - ❏ deepening my belief in God
   - ❏ other: _____

"To cling to my natural virtues is quite sufficient to obscure the work of God in me."
—Oswald Chambers

10. What is your reaction to this Scripture?
   ❐ I need to stop trying to be someone who does it all.
   ❐ I need to be more well-rounded in my skills, as this woman was.
   ❐ I need to have more of this woman's devotion to family.
   ❐ I need to have more of this woman's business savvy and skill.
   ❐ I need to focus less on beauty and more on faith in God.
   ❐ other: _____

11. What reward do you think this woman has earned?
   ❐ financial gain   ❐ a good reputation
   ❐ a month-long vacation   ❐ other: _____
   ❐ respect from those around her
   ❐ God's approval, love, and grace

 # CARING TIME / 15–45 Minutes / All Together

Leader: In this first session, take some time to discuss your expectations and to decide on the ground rules for your group. Then spend the remaining time in caring support for each other through sharing and prayer.

EXPECTATIONS

1. What motivated you to come to this group?
   ❐ curiosity
   ❐ A friend asked me.
   ❐ I had nothing better to do.
   ❐ a nagging suspicion that I'd better get my life together

2. As you begin this group, what are some goals or expectations you have for this course? Choose two or three of the following expectations and add one of your own:
   ❐ to discover what it means to be a godly woman
   ❐ to examine some biblical role models for women
   ❐ to strengthen my relationship with God
   ❐ to relax and forget about women's issues for awhile
   ❐ to see what the Bible has to say about womanhood
   ❐ to take an inventory of my life and learn skills to strengthen some areas
   ❐ to examine all facets of my life
   ❐ to discover new ways of pursuing a balanced life
   ❐ to understand how I can realize my full potential
   ❐ other: _____

3. If you could write your own ground rules for this group, what would you like to insist on? Choose any from the list below, and add one or two of your own:

   ❏ **Attendance:** To take the group seriously, and give the meetings priority.

   ❏ **Questions Encouraged:** This is a support group for people who are struggling with all sorts of questions, including questions about your your spiritual faith. Honest questions are encouraged.

   ❏ **Mission:** This group will be "open" to anyone who is struggling, and also to anyone who is seeking or who is starting over in the Christian life ... and it will be the mission of this group to invite new people to the sessions.

   ❏ **Accountability:** This group will be a support group. Prayer requests will be shared at the end of every session and group members will be encouraged to call each other to ask, "How's it going?"

   ❏ **Confidentiality:** Anything that is said in the group is kept in confidence.

   ❏ **Covenant:** At the end of this course, the group will evaluate the experience and decide if they wish to continue as a covenant group.

SHARING

Take a few minutes to share prayer requests with other group members. Go around and answer this question first:

"How can we help you in prayer this week?"

PRAYER

Take a moment to pray together. If you have not prayed out loud before, finish the sentence:

"Hello, God, this is ... (first name). I want to thank you for ..."

ACTION

1. You now have a brief overview of what it means to be a godly or virtuous woman. Write down two or three areas of concern you have about achieving this in your life. Refer to these during the next six weeks, praying that you will discover answers to your concerns.

2. Decide on where the group is going to meet.

3. Ask someone to bring refreshments next week.

4. Encourage the group to invite a friend to the group next week—to fill the "empty chair" (see page 5).

SESSION 2
Pursuing Balance

PURPOSE | To discover ways to balance a career and a home life.

AGENDA | **Gathering**    **Bible Study**   **Caring Time**

OPEN | **GATHERING / 15 Minutes / All Together**
Leader: The purpose of the Gathering Time in this session is to help people get to know each other a bit better and share something personal about themselves. We encourage you to be the first one to share with the group. Then read Step Two and move on to the Bible Study.

Step One: HOW TO "READ" ME. We are all faced with choices throughout our day. For each category below, choose the answer most suited for you. After everyone has finished, place all of the books in the middle and randomly redistribute the books. Let each person read someone else's book and ask the group to guess whose book it is.

1. The magazine I prefer is:
   - ❐ *Time/Newsweek*
   - ❐ *Woman's Day*
   - ❐ *People*
   - ❐ any Christian publication
   - ❐ *Cosmopolitan*
   - ❐ *Better Homes and Gardens*
   - ❐ any computer magazine
   - ❐ any financial magazine

2. The type of television show I prefer is:
   - ❐ a documentary
   - ❐ a love story
   - ❐ the nightly news
   - ❐ MTV/VH-1/TNN
   - ❐ an old movie
   - ❐ *Entertainment Tonight*
   - ❐ a drama
   - ❐ C-Span
   - ❐ a sitcom
   - ❐ a soap opera

3. The type of book I prefer is:
   - ❐ a mystery
   - ❐ good fiction
   - ❐ self-improvement
   - ❐ a religious book
   - ❐ poetry/a classic
   - ❐ a romance novel
   - ❐ non-fiction
   - ❐ an autobiography
   - ❐ science fiction
   - ❐ Who has time to read?

Step Two: PURSUING BALANCE. A woman's life has become more complicated in the last half of this century. The assumption was that a woman's life (apart from those who became teachers or nurses) would center around homemaking. Although many women found these limitations restricting, at least the expectations were simple. Today's woman is expected to do it all. In a commercial a few years back, a supposed prototype of today's woman sang, "I can bring home the bacon, fry it up in a pan," and in the midst of it all never let her husband "forget that he is a man." No wonder many of us think we need a red "S" printed on our chest.

But others of us pursue a balance between our personal lives and our jobs, or between our careers and our children. Or we simply try to balance all the demands of life in the '90s with time for ourselves. Whereas society encourages a personal pursuit of emotional and physical health (see Session 3), little is said about pursuing knowledge. There is a tendency in our society (and in many churches) to feel that once we reach a certain age, we no longer have to learn. But we are taught in Scripture to pursue learning. For this brings balance to our lives. Not only are we to grow in our faith, but also in knowledge as a whole.

LEADER:
Choose the
OPTION 1 Bible
Study (below)
or the OPTION 2
Study (page 17).

In this session, we will be looking at two women who pursued balance in their lives. In the Option One Study (from the book of First Kings), we will consider the story of the Queen of Sheba, who visited King Solomon. She was a woman who had a passion for knowledge and learning, and who benefited from being in the marketplace. In the Option Two Study (from the Acts of the Apostles), we will look at the life of Lydia and her ability to balance her home, business, and her thirst for spiritual truth.

 # BIBLE STUDY / 30 Minutes / Groups of 4
Leader: If you have more than seven in this session, we recommend groups of four—but not the same foursomes as last week. Ask one person in each foursome to be the Convener and complete the Bible Study in the time allotted. Remember, you have two choices for Bible Study: Option One and Option Two. Then regather for the Caring Time, allowing 20 minutes.

OPTION 1

Old Testament Study / Queen of Sheeba
1 Kings 10:1–10, 13

STUDY

Read 1 Kings 10:1–10, 13 and discuss the questions which follow with your group. This story occurred during the reign of King Solomon.

10 *When the queen of Sheba heard about the fame of Solomon and his relation to the name of the LORD, she came to test him with hard questions. ²Arriving at Jerusalem with a very great caravan—with camels carrying spices, large quantities of gold, and precious stones—she came to Solomon and talked with him about all that she had on her mind. ³Solomon answered all her questions; nothing was too hard for the king to explain to her. ⁴When the queen of Sheba saw all the wisdom of Solomon and the palace he had built, ⁵the food on his table, the seating of his officials, the attending servants in their robes, his cupbearers, and the burnt offerings he made at the temple of the LORD, she was overwhelmed.*

⁶She said to the king, "The report I heard in my own country about your achievements and your wisdom is true. ⁷But I did not believe these things until I came and saw with my own eyes. Indeed, not even half was told me; in wisdom and wealth you have far exceeded the report I heard. ⁸How happy your men must be! How happy your officials, who continually stand before you and hear your wisdom! ⁹Praise be to the LORD your God, who has delighted in you and placed you on the throne of Israel. Because of the LORD's eternal love for Israel, he has made you king, to maintain justice and righteousness."

¹⁰And she gave the king 120 talents of gold, large quantities of spices, and precious stones. Never again were so many spices brought in as those the queen of Sheba gave to King Solomon. ...

¹³King Solomon gave the queen of Sheba all she desired and asked for, besides what he had given her out of his royal bounty. Then she left and returned with her retinue to her own country.

1 Kings 10:1–10, 13, NIV

1. What impresses you the most about the queen of Sheba?
   - ❏ that she was knowledgeable enough to ask such intelligent questions of Solomon and understand his answers (v. 3)
   - ❏ that she was a woman of many means and resources (v. 10)
   - ❏ that she knew how to flatter Solomon (vv. 6–8)
   - ❏ that she was willing to praise Solomon's God (v. 9)
   - ❏ that she "saw" wisdom (v. 7)

"As knowledge increases, wonder deepens."
—Charles Morgany

2. Finish this sentence: "The queen of Sheba probably complimented Solomon so profusely because ..."
   - ❏ he was handsome and she was after his attention.
   - ❏ she was trying to make a business deal with him.
   - ❏ she had no self-worth and she was groveling before a man.
   - ❏ she was trying to manipulate him through his male ego.
   - ❏ she was sincerely impressed with him.

3. Who truly admires you or seeks out your opinion?

LEADER: When you have completed the Bible Study, move on to the Caring Time (page 20).

4. If you could have an audience with the wisest person of our day, whom would you choose? What question would you ask them?

5. The queen of Sheba pursued knowledge. Choose an item from the list below which keeps you from pursuing knowledge in your life:
   ❒ time with family   ❒ demands from my spouse
   ❒ television   ❒ laziness—an undisciplined mind
   ❒ other: _____

6. Which of the following perspectives about women and men in the business world come to your mind as you read this story?
   ❒ To succeed, women have to "kiss up" to men.
   ❒ Solomon was like a lot of men today—they feel they have to lecture you because of their "wisdom."
   ❒ This shows men and women can coexist in the business world.
   ❒ The queen of Sheba was, and should be, an aberration—business is for men.
   ❒ Women can be in business—but it's okay to show respect for male accomplishment.

7. How would you feel if you were a wealthy, influential wheeler-dealer like the queen of Sheba?
   ❒ It's my life's dream.
   ❒ It would be nice—but only if I don't have to give up too much time with those I care about.
   ❒ I'm not sure—I want it and I don't.
   ❒ This has no appeal to me—give me a secure home and a working man.

8. If someone could give you "all you desired and asked for," what would it be? Prioritize the following options from "1" (highest priority) to "10" (lowest priority):
   __ great wealth   __ happy children
   __ obedient children   __ a happy spouse
   __ a successful career   __ a sense of purpose in my work
   __ a life of minimum stress   __ a close walk with God
   __ a group of intimate and reliable friends
   __ making a significant contribution to the world

9. What do these priorities indicate about the next steps you need to take in your life?

The queen of Sheba was the first reigning queen on record who pitted her wits and wealth against those of a king. It is hard to believe that nine centuries before Christ, Sabean women occupied such a high place as did the queen of Sheba. The International Standard Bible Encyclopedia states that "in almost all respects, women appeared to have been considered the equal of men and to have discharged the same civil, religious, and even military functions."

Her riches were substantial: the 120 talents of gold she presented to King Solomon would be worth about $3.6 million. Perhaps the main purpose of her trip was to negotiate a trade agreement with Solomon. At the time, he controlled the trade routes. His control jeopardized the income which the Sabeans were used to receiving from the caravans which crossed the country.

She had a great thirst for knowledge and went to the wisest person she knew of at the time. She was one of many rulers who sought King Solomon's wisdom. While others sent ambassadors, she traveled the 1,200 miles herself. She was a courageous, resourceful woman, who took an active part in increasing the prosperity of her own people.

OPTION 2

New Testament Study / Lydia
Acts 16:11–15

STUDY

Lydia was a woman of Thyatira. Lydia was a businesswoman, a "dealer of purple cloth," and was probably one of the most successful and influential women of Philippi. Read Acts 16:11–15 and share your responses to the following questions with your group.

> *11From Troas we put out to sea and sailed straight for Samothrace, and the next day on to Neapolis. 12From there we traveled to Philippi, a Roman colony and the leading city of that district of Macedonia. And we stayed there several days.*
>
> *13On the Sabbath we went outside the city gate to the river, where we expected to find a place of prayer. We sat down and began to speak to the women who had gathered there. 14One of those listening was a woman named Lydia, a dealer in purple cloth from the city of Thyatira, who was a worshiper of God. The Lord opened her heart to respond to Paul's message. 15When she and the members of her household were baptized, she invited us to her home. "If you consider me a believer in the Lord," she said, "come and stay at my house." And she persuaded us.*
>
> ***Acts 16:11–15, NIV***

1. Which of the following words best describes your first impression of Lydia as you meet her in this story?
   - ❐ persuasive
   - ❐ spiritual
   - ❐ trusting
   - ❐ industrious
   - ❐ hospitable
   - ❐ impulsive
   - ❐ naive
   - ❐ friendly

2. As a little girl, what did you want to be when you grew up?
   - ❐ a princess
   - ❐ a businesswoman
   - ❐ a nurse
   - ❐ a movie star
   - ❐ a scientist
   - ❐ a ballerina
   - ❐ a teacher
   - ❐ a doctor
   - ❐ a famous athlete
   - ❐ other: _____

3. Which of the following do you find most impressive about Lydia?
   - ❐ She was a businesswoman at a time when few women were.
   - ❐ She took time out of her business to go to a women's prayer group.
   - ❐ She had enough influence over her household to convince them to be baptized.
   - ❐ She was willing to open her home to strangers.

4. Lydia was studying the Scriptures by the river. In what environment do you learn best?
   - ❐ alone in a secluded place
   - ❐ in the library
   - ❐ in front of the computer
   - ❐ in a classroom
   - ❐ in front of the television
   - ❐ sitting around talking with others in a casual setting
   - ❐ in my "comfy" chair with a cup of coffee
   - ❐ outside in natural surroundings
   - ❐ other: _____

5. From her behavior in this story, what would you say was Lydia's feeling about home? How would you describe your attitude toward home?
   - ❐ Home is a place to retreat from other people.
   - ❐ Home is a place to share with other people.
   - ❐ Home is just a convenient place to do business.
   - ❐ Home is where you focus on family first.
   - ❐ Home is where you focus on yourself first.
   - ❐ Home is where you go when you have nowhere better to go.
   - ❐ other: _____

6. Lydia was a businesswoman who sold purple cloth. What type of business have you dreamed of starting?

"The most worthwhile form of education is the kind that puts the educator inside you, as it were, so that the appetite for learning persists long after the external pressure for grades and degrees has vanished. Otherwise you are not educated; you are merely trained."
—Sydney J. Harris

7. What is preventing you from fulfilling your dream?
   - ❏ time
   - ❏ money
   - ❏ fear of failure
   - ❏ my family obligations
   - ❏ inability to risk
   - ❏ lack of support
   - ❏ I'm not sure I'm intelligent enough to pull it off.
   - ❏ I don't know how to dream anymore.
   - ❏ other: _____

8. Lydia managed to pay attention to her business (v. 14), her spiritual life (v. 14), and her household (v. 15). How would you rate yourself in each of those areas?

   my business/professional life:

1	2	3	4	5	6	7	8	9	10
a real washout				**making do**			**succeeding superbly**		

   my spiritual life:

1	2	3	4	5	6	7	8	9	10
a real washout				**making do**			**succeeding superbly**		

   at home:

1	2	3	4	5	6	7	8	9	10
a real washout				**making do**			**succeeding superbly**		

9. What is the next step you should take to put your home, work, and a spiritual life in better balance?

LEADER: When you have completed the Bible Study, move on to the Caring Time (page 20).

10. Lydia risked her business and reputation in order to learn more about God. On a scale of 1 to 10 (1= I'm not willing to risk anything to 10= I'm willing to risk everything), what level of risk are you willing to take to grow in your faith?

1	2	3	4	5	6	7	8	9	10
I won't risk anything.							**I'll risk everything.**		

COMMENT

Lydia was obviously a woman of some importance. The purple dye, which Lydia traded, was well-known throughout the world. More than that, she was a seeker of truth, and became Paul's first convert in Philippi.

Lydia was evidently a woman of determination, foresight, and generosity. She and other women met on the banks of the river for peace and quiet and prayer. Lydia was a Jewish proselyte, a Gentile who worshiped the God of the Jews. Because of Lydia's great desire to know more about the wonders and power of God, she was at this place of prayer by the river. We can assume that this little prayer group had asked for guidance. Paul and his companions came to the river on this particular Sabbath. As Lydia listened to Paul, we are told that the Lord opened her heart. Soon afterward, Lydia and others (possibly from her household or her business) were baptized. Her decision to convert to Christianity was made regardless of the possible ramifications to her business.

After her baptism, Lydia expressed her desire to know more about Christ. She showed Paul, Luke, and Silas great hospitality. She was head of the household, which in those days meant she was probably unmarried or widowed. She even opened her doors to Paul and Silas when they were later released from prison (Acts 16:40).

 ## CARING TIME / 15–45 Minutes / All Together
Leader: The purpose of the Caring Time in this session is to spend time in caring support for each other through Sharing, Prayer and Action.

SHARING

Share with the group:

> *What help do you need from this group to take the "next steps" you have said you need to take to balance your world?*

PRAYER

Gather your group in a circle and pray for the concerns and struggles voiced during this meeting. If you would like to pray in silence, say the word "Amen" when you finish, so that the next person will know when to start.

ACTION

Talk with a working woman outside of this group whom you admire or look up to. Ask her how she manages to balance the demands of work and home.

SESSION 3
Pursuing Wholeness

To discover ways to gain emotional and physical health.

    **Gathering**    **Bible Study**    **Caring Time**

    ## GATHERING / 15 Minutes / All Together
Leader: Read the instructions for Step One and set the pace by going first. Then read the Introduction in Step Two and move on to the Bible Study.

Step One: WHAT I NEED RIGHT NOW. Choose five items from this list that you think you need more of in your life. Tell the group why you chose what you did. (This list is adapted from *Structured Exercises in Wellness Promotion*, Tubesing and Tubesing, eds., Whole Person Press, 1983.)

strength	self-esteem	caring
composure	security	recognition
balance	activity	confidence
awareness	health	motivation
solitude	devotion	sharing
trust	comfort	joy
communion	accomplishments	forgiveness
faith	purpose	celebration
support	responsibility	commitment
romance	intimacy	patience
sensitivity	childlikeness	sleep
challenges	exercise	laughter
control	imagination	money
education	flexibility	freedom
energy	self-control	relaxation
nutrition	touching	other: _____

Step Two: PURSUING WHOLENESS. Although we weren't reared in an age of health-consciousness, we certainly live in such an age today. We are constantly reminded to watch what we eat, lower our cholesterol level, monitor the number of fat grams we eat, exercise daily, etc. We are also reminded of the emotional healing which needs to take place. It is now estimated that one out of every three women has been abused in her lifetime. Abuse (whether physical or emotional) is a national epidemic. Or as some would argue it has been a national epidemic which is only now coming to light. The fact remains that most of us need physical or emotional healing. Hopefully, we don't have a life-threatening disease or aren't a victim of sexual abuse. But we still need to take care of our bodies, watch our health, and learn additional healthy ways to deal with our emotions.

LEADER:
Choose the
OPTION 1 Bible
Study (below) of
the OPTION 2
Study (page 25).

In Option One, we will study the passage of Bathsheba. She was a victim of abuse, who received healing in her life and was restored to wholeness. In Option Two we will study the passage of the woman with the issue of blood, who sought physical healing from Christ. Remember, the point of these Bible Studies is to share your concerns about physical and emotional healing. Please be aware of the sensitive nature of this study.

BIBLE STUDY / 30 Minutes / Groups of 4

Leader: Help the group decide on Option One or Option Two for their Bible Study. If there are 7 or more in the group, encourage them to move into groups of 4. Ask one person in each group to be the Convener. The Convener guides the sharing and makes sure that each group member has an opportunity to answer every question.

OPTION 1

Old Testament Study / Bathsheba
2 Samuel 11:1–5, 14–17, 26–27

STUDY

Read 2 Samuel 11:1–5, 14–17, and 26–27 and the Comment section (page 25). Then discuss your responses to the following questions with the group.

11 *In the spring, at the time when kings go off to war, David sent Joab out with the king's men and the whole Israelite army. They destroyed the Ammonites and besieged Rabbah. But David remained in Jerusalem.*

²One evening David got up from his bed and walked around on the roof of the palace. From the roof he saw a woman bathing. The woman was very beautiful, ³and David sent someone to find out about her. The man said, "Isn't this Bathsheba, the daughter of Eliam and the wife of Uriah the Hittite?" ⁴Then David sent messengers to get her. She came to him, and he slept with her. (She had purified herself from her uncleanness.) Then she went back home. ⁵The woman conceived and sent word to David, saying, "I am pregnant. ..."

14In the morning David wrote a letter to Joab and sent it with Uriah. 15In it he wrote, "Put Uriah in the front line where the fighting is fiercest. Then withdraw from him so he will be struck down and die."

16So while Joab had the city under siege, he put Uriah at a place where he knew the strongest defenders were. 17When the men of the city came out and fought against Joab, some of the men in David's army fell; moreover, Uriah the Hittite died. ...

26When Uriah's wife heard that her husband was dead, she mourned for him. 27After the time of mourning was over, David had her brought to his house, and she became his wife and bore him a son. But the thing David had done displeased the LORD.

2 Samuel 11:1–5, 14–17, 26–27, NIV

1. Imagine that this scandal had occurred today between a woman and a major political figure. Which of the following scenarios do you think would have happened?
   ❑ Everyone would say, "Ho, hum—again?"
   ❑ The politician would rely on "plausible deniability."
   ❑ The woman would be cast as a bimbo and the villainess.
   ❑ The politician would write about it and have a best-seller.
   ❑ It would be one of those scandals that fades from the news.

2. What is your reaction to Bathsheba's visit to the king's palace?
   ❑ She was a coward for going.
   ❑ I pity her.
   ❑ I can't believe she would do something that dumb.
   ❑ She didn't have a choice.
   ❑ I probably would have done the same thing.

3. If you could put in a good word for Bathsheba, what would you say?
   ❑ She turned a horrible situation into a good thing.
   ❑ She was a great advocate for her son.
   ❑ She couldn't help what happened to her.
   ❑ She was only human.
   ❑ She was confused.

4. What do you think Bathsheba did after David slept with her?
   ❑ told her family or a close friend what happened
   ❑ poured her heart out to God
   ❑ kept everything inside her
   ❑ looked at her options and tried to hold David accountable
   ❑ looked out for her son's future
   ❑ decided to use the situation to her advantage

"If you have made mistakes, even serious mistakes, there is always another chance for you. And supposing you have tried and failed again and again, you may have a fresh start at any moment you choose, for this one thing that we call 'failure' is not the falling down, but the staying down."
—Mary Pickford

5. What do you think Bathsheba felt as her identity quickly changed from Uriah's wife, to David's fling, to Uriah's widow, to David's bride?
   - ❏ overwhelmed—her head kept spinning
   - ❏ grieving—for all her losses
   - ❏ fear—what will happen next?
   - ❏ anger—that God would allow this to happen to her
   - ❏ depressed—when will life be normal again?

6. Who would you have identified with most in this story when you were an adolescent?
   - ❏ David, because I would get into trouble and make it worse by trying to cover it up
   - ❏ Bathsheba, because I was pressured into doing what I didn't want to do
   - ❏ Bathsheba, because guys would take advantage of me
   - ❏ Uriah, because I was often the one betrayed

7. If you were in Bathsheba's situation today, how would you react?
   - ❏ angry at God
   - ❏ depressed
   - ❏ do penance
   - ❏ forget about it
   - ❏ run away from the situation
   - ❏ hide my feelings from everyone
   - ❏ ask for forgiveness and move on
   - ❏ other: _____

8. If a good friend of yours was in an abusive situation, what advice would you give her?
   - ❏ hang in there—God will not abandon you
   - ❏ get out of the situation immediately
   - ❏ you must have done something that brought this on yourself
   - ❏ in time you will be able to turn the negative into a positive
   - ❏ other: _____

LEADER: When you have completed the Bible Study, move on to the Caring Time (page 28).

9. Bathsheba mourned the loss of Uriah. What loss do you mourn?
   - ❏ like Bathsheba—the loss of a relationship
   - ❏ some mistakes I made a long time ago
   - ❏ a mistake I made recently
   - ❏ some bad relationships with men
   - ❏ the experiences with family I have given up in order to work
   - ❏ the professional opportunities I missed by having a family
   - ❏ the dream of finishing my degree
   - ❏ other: _____

According to the law, Bathsheba could not have resisted David even if she wanted to, for a woman in ancient times was completely subject to the king's will. If King David desired her, he could have her. Today a relationship is considered to be abusive whenever a person who has power over someone else (such as a boss over an employee, a teacher over a student, or a minister over a parishioner) has extramarital sex with that person. Such was certainly the case with Bathsheba. After David abused her, all she could do was go home. We do not get any indication from the biblical text as to Bathsheba's feelings were. She simply sends a message to him that she is pregnant.

David then tries to avoid a scandal by arranging to send Uriah home from the war to his wife. But Uriah refuses—he will not have relations with his wife while he is a soldier and his country is at war. At this point, David arranges for Uriah's inevitable death on the battlefield. The crime was David's, but Bathsheba suffered the consequences of it. We observe her pain as she grieves the loss of her husband. Her grief is compounded by the death of the baby she had with David. But after an appropriate time of mourning, David takes her as his wife.

Bathsheba continues recovering from her abuse. She bears David four sons: Solomon (whose name means "the peaceful"), Shimea, Shobab, and Nathan. As the mother of King Solomon, Bathsheba takes an honored place among women in the Bible (Matthew 1:6). There is no record of her during Solomon's youth. However, when King David is old and dying, she carried out the most important mission of her life. Bathsheba intervened to have her son Solomon succeed his father as king of Israel (1 Kings 1:17–21). She showed wisdom, finesse, courtesy, and vision. Only an intelligent and respected woman, in whom the aged king had great confidence, could have won such a great victory (1 Kings 1:29–30). And only a much-loved mother could receive the place of honor as queen mother on the king's right side, a place of power and authority.

OPTION 2

New Testament Study / Woman with the Issue of Blood
Luke 8:42b–48

STUDY

This woman was unnamed by the gospel writers. But she was important enough for Jesus to interrupt his routine. Undoubtedly, this woman was weak and disheartened. Even Luke, a physician, admitted that no doctor could heal her. Read Luke 8:42b–48 and discuss your responses to the following questions with your group.

As Jesus was on his way, the crowds almost crushed him. ⁴³And a woman was there who had been subject to bleeding for twelve years, but no one could heal her. ⁴⁴She came up behind him and touched the edge of his cloak, and immediately her bleeding stopped.

⁴⁵"Who touched me?" Jesus asked.

When they all denied it, Peter said, "Master, the people are crowding and pressing against you."

⁴⁶But Jesus said, "Someone touched me; I know that power has gone out from me."

⁴⁷Then the woman, seeing that she could not go unnoticed, came trembling and fell at his feet. In the presence of all the people, she told why she had touched him and how she had been instantly healed. ⁴⁸Then he said to her, "Daughter, your faith has healed you. Go in peace."

Luke 8:42b–48, NIV

1. What is the most significant aspect of this story to you?
   ❐ that Jesus delayed helping a wealthy man in order to heal a common woman
   ❐ that this woman tried to be healed again after all her failures
   ❐ that Jesus paid attention to an individual in a crowd
   ❐ that the woman was healed just by touching Jesus' garment

2. Why did Jesus insist on finding the person who had touched him?
   ❐ He wanted her to witness to others.
   ❐ He wanted her to know he noticed her as an individual.
   ❐ He wanted to point out to her what her *faith* had done.
   ❐ He thought she might need further healing.

3. This woman, like many persons in the New Testament, was healed by physical touch. Mark on the scale below what the attitude was toward physical touch in the home where you grew up:

1	2	3	4	5	6	7	8	9	10
Touching was considered bad.				We hugged on special occasions				We were a very "huggy" family	

4. Why do you think this woman secretly came up from behind Jesus instead of going to him directly for the healing she wanted?
   ❐ She could tell he was busy, and didn't want to bother him.
   ❐ She didn't like crowds and didn't want attention.
   ❐ She didn't want publicly to admit her need.
   ❐ She was used to failure and didn't want to get her hopes up.

5. When have you been as desperate as this woman?
   - ❏ as a child
   - ❏ when I was in college
   - ❏ as a young wife/mother
   - ❏ as a teenager
   - ❏ I feel that desperate now.
   - ❏ I've never felt that desperate.

6. How did Jesus "touch" you at your time of desperation?
   - ❏ I felt his presence and became more calm.
   - ❏ I felt his presence and his peace.
   - ❏ He helped me figure out the best course of action.
   - ❏ He sent someone to be with me.
   - ❏ He literally healed me through miraculous means.
   - ❏ He healed me through the skills of doctors.
   - ❏ I never sensed Jesus' touch.

7. What connections have you noticed between your physical and spiritual health?
   - ❏ My physical health only lasts if I am spiritually well.
   - ❏ My physical health is sometimes related to my spiritual health.
   - ❏ My physical health is sometimes helped by spiritual remedies.
   - ❏ A prayer a day keeps the doctor away.
   - ❏ I don't see a connection.

8. Imagine that you were with Jesus in the crowds today. What would you ask him to heal you from?
   - ❏ a physical illness
   - ❏ a family problem
   - ❏ a personal problem
   - ❏ an emotional illness
   - ❏ a spiritual problem
   - ❏ other: _____

9. The word "peace" (v. 48) is the Greek word for *shalom* or complete harmony (spiritual, emotional, in every way). What do you think this word meant to this woman at that moment in her life?
   - ❏ Her life wasn't over yet.
   - ❏ God had not disowned her.
   - ❏ It was okay to feel discouraged, but there was a new day ahead.
   - ❏ It probably didn't mean much to her.
   - ❏ It was probably the first real words of hope she had heard in 12 years.

10. What does the word "peace" (*shalom*) mean to you?

LEADER: When you have completed the Bible Study, move on to the Caring Time (page 28).

COMMENT

According to the law at the time, this woman was regarded as unclean and was therefore restricted in her contact with others. How could she dare to venture out into the crowds and find Jesus? But she believed deep in her heart that if she touched his garment, she would be healed. And when she gently touched the edge of his clothing, she immediately felt his healing power go through her body. But Jesus also felt her touch, and since he knew that it was more than the casual contact of the crowds, he asked who touched him. Even though she was fearful of what he might say (but at the same time overcome with joy because she was healed), she pushed her way forward and admitted that she was the one who had touched him.

Instead of a rebuke, she receives words of encouragement, comfort, and hope. She would remain physically healed because of her faith. And she would be whole as Jesus pronounced words of his peace.

 CARING TIME / 15–45 Minutes / All Together
Leader: Bring all of the foursomes back together for a time of caring. Follow the three steps below.

SHARING

Share a prayer request for yourself in the area of healing and wholeness. If you are comfortable, share a concern you have about a time when you were taken advantage of or abused, or a place where you need to experience God's healing in your life.

PRAYER

Gather your group in a circle and pray for the persons mentioned, as well as for other concerns shared in the meeting. If you would like to pray in silence, say the word "Amen" when you finish your prayer, so that the next person will know when to start.

ACTION

Remember your neighbor's prayer request throughout the week. Drop her a note of encouragement with respect to her prayer request.

SESSION 4
Pursuing Healthy Relationships

PURPOSE

To learn the keys to healthier relationships in life.

AGENDA

 **Gathering**    **Bible Study**    **Caring Time**

OPEN

 GATHERING / 15 Minutes / All Together

Leader: Read the instructions for Step One and set the pace by going first. Then read the Introduction in Step Two and move on to the Bible Study.

Step One: MY RELATIONSHIPS. How are you doing in your relationships? Choose a circle of relationships, such as your family, co-workers, or friends. Among the choices below, select the ones which best describe your recent behavior among the relationships you have chosen. Tell the group how you see yourself in those relationships, and how the other people in the relationships might have seen you.

- ❏ **Saint Sweetheart:** I couldn't be nicer.
- ❏ **Mickey Mouse:** I listen so much, I'm all ears!
- ❏ **A doormat:** People have been wiping their feet on me.
- ❏ **Teddy Bear:** I seem to comfort people.
- ❏ **A Grizzly Bear:** Watch out! I may bite!
- ❏ **Mother Hen:** Cluck! Cluck! Who needs me now?
- ❏ **Selfish Shellfish:** Keep your hands off my pearl!
- ❏ **The Grinch:** I seem to ruin everyone's fun.
- ❏ **St. Nick:** All I do is give, give, give.
- ❏ **Aladdin's Genie:** I can grant wishes!
- ❏ **Benedict Arnold:** I feel like a traitor.
- ❏ **Dracula:** People are afraid of me.

Step Two: PURSUING HEALTHY RELATIONSHIPS. We do not live in a vacuum. We do not live alone in this world, although at times we can feel very lonely. There is a big difference between "aloneness" and "loneliness." There are many people who live alone (due to being divorced, widowed, or choosing singleness) who aren't lonely. And the reverse is also true. There are many lonely people who live with others.

The only way to combat loneliness is to be in healthy relationships with others. Healthy relationships are balanced, where both parties involved are allowed and encouraged to be fully who they are. Healthy relationships require work—they don't just happen. As you can plant a seed in the ground (and are not guaranteed a harvest unless the plant is watered, fed, and cared for), so it is with healthy relationships. They need our time, attention, and energy in order to grow and remain healthy.

We have various relationships in our lives—with family members (spouses, parents, children, and relatives), friends, colleagues, neighbors, and acquaintances. All of these relationships are crucial in our attaining our fullest potential. The characteristics of a good and healthy friendship or marriage will apply to all of our relationships.

LEADER:
Choose the
OPTION 1 Bible
Study (below)
or the OPTION 2
Study (page 33).

In the following Option One Study (from the book of Ruth), we will see the story of one of the great (and loyal) relationships of all time between two women. And in Option Two (from Luke's Gospel), we will examine how the relationships between Elizabeth and Zechariah and Elizabeth and Mary can be viewed as models for our relationships as well.

BIBLE STUDY / 30 Minutes / Groups of 4

Leader: Help the groups decide on the Option One or Option Two Bible Study. If there are more than seven people, divide into groups of four, and ask one person in each group to be the Convener. Finish the Bible Study in 30 minutes, and gather the groups together for the Caring Time.

OPTION 1

Old Testament Study / Ruth and Naomi
Ruth 1:3–18

STUDY

Read Ruth 1:3–18 and discuss your responses to the following questions with your group. Ruth's words in verse 16 are often used in marriage ceremonies. But in this original context, they referred to a friendship between women, not a marriage. Because of Ruth's loyalty, however, she did eventually meet her future husband, Boaz. As a couple, they were ancestors of King David (and eventually of Christ himself).

³Now Elimelech, Naomi's husband, died, and she was left with her two sons. ⁴They married Moabite women, one named Orpah and the other Ruth. After they had lived there about ten years, ⁵both Mahlon and Kilion also died, and Naomi was left without her two sons and her husband.

⁶When she heard in Moab that the LORD had come to the aid of his people by providing food for them, Naomi and her daughters-in-law prepared to return home from there. ⁷With her two daughters-in-law she left the place where she had been living and set out on the road that would take them back to the land of Judah.

⁸Then Naomi said to her two daughters-in-law, "Go back, each of you, to your mother's home. May the LORD show kindness to you, as you have shown to your dead and to me. ⁹May the LORD grant that each of you will find rest in the home of another husband."

Then she kissed them and they wept aloud ¹⁰and said to her, "We will go back with you to your people."

¹¹But Naomi said, "Return home, my daughters. Why would you come with me? Am I going to have any more sons, who could become your husbands? ¹²Return home, my daughters; I am too old to have another husband. Even if I thought there was still hope for me—even if I had a husband tonight and then gave birth to sons—¹³would you wait until they grew up? Would you remain unmarried for them? No, my daughters. It is more bitter for me than for you, because the LORD's hand has gone out against me!"

¹⁴At this they wept again. Then Orpah kissed her mother-in-law good-by, but Ruth clung to her.

¹⁵"Look," said Naomi, "your sister-in-law is going back to her people and her gods. Go back with her."

¹⁶But Ruth replied, "Don't urge me to leave you or to turn back from you. Where you go I will go, and where you stay I will stay. Your people will be my people and your God my God. ¹⁷Where you die I will die, and there I will be buried. May the LORD deal with me, be it ever so severely, if anything but death separates you and me." ¹⁸When Naomi realized that Ruth was determined to go with her, she stopped urging her.

Ruth 1:3–18, NIV

1. Which of the following modern songs would you choose to describe the friendship of Ruth and Naomi?
   - ❏ "Wind Beneath My Wings" by Bette Midler
   - ❏ "People (Who Need People)" by Barbra Streisand
   - ❏ "That's What Friends Are For" by Dionne Warwick
   - ❏ "You've Got A Friend" by James Taylor
   - ❏ "We Are Family" by Sly and the Family Stone

2. Why did Naomi ask her daughters-in-law to go back to their own people?
   - ❏ She was deeply immersed in self-pity.
   - ❏ She was tired of them and wanted to get rid of them gently.
   - ❏ She was testing them to see if they really wanted to go with her.
   - ❏ She was concerned for their welfare.

3. Why did Ruth decide to stay with Naomi?
- ❏ She probably didn't get along with her own mother.
- ❏ She felt obligated to watch out for her.
- ❏ She was an adventuresome sort and wanted to travel.
- ❏ She was intensely loyal to those she cared about.
- ❏ She knew Naomi could vouch for her to male relatives.
- ❏ She had become dependent on Naomi.

4. When you were in grade school who did you follow (or who followed you) wherever he or she went? What made this relationship special?

5. At what point do you really identify with the events in this story?
- ❏ I also have lost a husband. (v. 5)
- ❏ I have wondered, as Naomi did, why anyone would want to be with me. (v. 11)
- ❏ I have sent people away who wanted to stay with me.
- ❏ I have felt closer to my mother-in-law than to my own mother.
- ❏ I have had someone to stay with me during tough times.
- ❏ I have stayed with someone during tough times.

6. What is the closest you have come to having a relationship like this one between Ruth and Naomi?

7. What needs to happen in a relationship before you have the spirit of Ruth and are willing to stay with the person no matter what?
- ❏ They need to have stayed with me in the past
- ❏ We need to have shared our deepest feelings.
- ❏ We need to have had a history together—shared experiences.
- ❏ We need to be family.
- ❏ We need to have a certain "chemistry" with each other.
- ❏ We need to have gone through some hard times together.
- ❏ I'll show such loyalty to anyone.
- ❏ other: _____

LEADER: When you have completed the Bible Study, move on to the Caring Time (page 37).

8. What troubling experience are you facing now where you need someone "to go with you"?
- ❏ a health crisis
- ❏ a relational crisis
- ❏ a vocational crisis
- ❏ a spiritual crisis
- ❏ a crisis of my identity as a woman
- ❏ I don't see anything troubling ahead of me.

New Testament Study / Elizabeth
Luke 1:5–7, 11–18, 23–25, 39–45, 57–66

STUDY

Read these verses from the first chapter of Luke's Gospel and discuss the questions which follow with your group. In this passage, we will study the relationship between Elizabeth and her husband, Zechariah; and the relationship between Elizabeth and her cousin, Mary.

⁵In the time of Herod king of Judea there was a priest named Zechariah, who belonged to the priestly division of Abijah; his wife Elizabeth was also a descendant of Aaron. ⁶Both of them were upright in the sight of God, observing all the Lord's commandments and regulations blamelessly. ⁷But they had no children, because Elizabeth was barren; and they were both well along in years. ...

¹¹Then an angel of the Lord appeared to him, standing at the right side of the altar of incense. ¹²When Zechariah saw him, he was startled and was gripped with fear. ¹³But the angel said to him: "Do not be afraid, Zechariah; your prayer has been heard. Your wife Elizabeth will bear you a son, and you are to give him the name John. ¹⁴He will be a joy and delight to you, and many will rejoice because of his birth, ¹⁵for he will be great in the sight of the Lord. He is never to take wine or other fermented drink, and he will be filled with the Holy Spirit even from birth. ¹⁶Many of the people of Israel will he bring back to the Lord their God. ¹⁷And he will go on before the Lord, in the spirit and power of Elijah, to turn the hearts of the fathers to their children and the disobedient to the wisdom of the righteous—to make ready a people prepared for the Lord."

¹⁸Zechariah asked the angel, "How can I be sure of this? I am an old man and my wife is well along in years." ...

²³When his time of service was completed, he returned home. ²⁴After this his wife Elizabeth became pregnant and for five months remained in seclusion. ²⁵"The Lord has done this for me," she said. "In these days he has shown his favor and taken away my disgrace among the people." ...

³⁹At that time Mary got ready and hurried to a town in the hill country of Judea, ⁴⁰where she entered Zechariah's home and greeted Elizabeth. ⁴¹When Elizabeth heard Mary's greeting, the baby leaped in her womb, and Elizabeth was filled with the Holy Spirit. ⁴²In a loud voice she exclaimed: "Blessed are you among women, and blessed is the child you will bear! ⁴³But why am I so favored, that the mother of my Lord should come to me? ⁴⁴As soon as the sound of your greeting reached my ears, the baby in my womb leaped for joy. ⁴⁵Blessed is she who has believed that what the Lord has said to her will be accomplished!" ...

⁵⁷When it was time for Elizabeth to have her baby, she gave birth to a son. ⁵⁸Her neighbors and relatives heard that the Lord had shown her great mercy, and they shared her joy.

⁵⁹On the eighth day they came to circumcise the child, and they were going to name him after his father Zechariah, ⁶⁰but his mother spoke up and said, "No! He is to be called John."

⁶¹They said to her, "There is no one among your relatives who has that name."

⁶²Then they made signs to his father, to find out what he would like to name the child. ⁶³He asked for a writing tablet, and to everyone's astonishment he wrote, "His name is John." ⁶⁴Immediately his mouth was opened and his tongue was loosed, and he began to speak, praising God. ⁶⁵The neighbors were all filled with awe, and throughout the hill country of Judea people were talking about all these things. ⁶⁶Everyone who heard this wondered about it, asking, "What then is this child going to be?" For the Lord's hand was with him.

Luke 1:5–7, 11–18, 23–25, 39–45, 57–66, NIV

1. Which part of this passage is the most difficult for you to understand?
   - ❑ that Elizabeth could give birth after years of being barren
   - ❑ that although he was a godly man and a priest, Zechariah would not believe the angel
   - ❑ that Elizabeth and Mary were pregnant at the same time
   - ❑ that Zechariah agreed with Elizabeth concerning the naming of their son
   - ❑ I don't have a hard time with any of it.
   - ❑ other: _____

2. With whom do you identify most in this story? Least? Why?
   - ❑ Zechariah (early)—I have been faithful to God for a long time, but feel I haven't received some of the fringe benefits.
   - ❑ Zechariah (later)—I too have doubted God's promises to me.
   - ❑ Elizabeth—I anxiously wait for God to hear and answer my innermost prayers.
   - ❑ John—I feel that God has special plans for me.
   - ❑ the angel—Sometimes people don't believe me when I tell them something.
   - ❑ Mary—I enjoy sharing my good news/fortune with others.
   - ❑ other: _____

3. Barrenness was viewed as a sign of God's disfavor and was a legitimate reason for divorce. What feelings might Zechariah and Elizabeth have had in light of their barrenness?
   - ❑ confusion—How could we live the way God wants us to and not have his favor?
   - ❑ frustration—What did we do wrong?
   - ❑ anger—This isn't fair, after all we have done for God!
   - ❑ hurt—I can't believe God would turn his back on us!
   - ❑ other: _____

"The healthiest relationships are those that breathe—that move out and then move back together."
—James Dobson

34

4. In what ways do you feel barren?
   - ❐ in my marriage
   - ❐ in my career
   - ❐ feeling fulfilled as a woman
   - ❐ in my relationships
   - ❐ in my spiritual life
   - ❐ other: _____

5. How might this account of Elizabeth and Zechariah affect your feelings of barrenness?
   - ❐ Their story gives me hope for the future.
   - ❐ I guess God hasn't abandoned me after all.
   - ❐ To be honest, I don't get a lot of comfort from this story.
   - ❐ I can't make the leap between our situations.
   - ❐ other: _____

6. Why did Mary go to Elizabeth's house?
   - ❐ for a little "female bonding"
   - ❐ to get away from the neighbors' talk about her pregnancy
   - ❐ to share in the joy of another pregnant woman
   - ❐ to get some advice from an older and wiser female relative
   - ❐ just to spread the exciting news

7. There was a special relationship between Elizabeth and Mary. What female friend do you have such a relationship with, and what makes your relationship special?

8. What things that Mary and Elizabeth did are important to you in a friendship?
   - ❐ a shared experience—but it doesn't have to be a pregnancy
   - ❐ really sharing in the other person's joy
   - ❐ taking time to visit each other
   - ❐ talking about our feelings
   - ❐ encouraging each other in the faith
   - ❐ non-competitiveness—like when Elizabeth wasn't jealous of who Mary's son would be

9. What do you need to share with an "Elizabeth" right now?
   - ❐ a joy that I have been wanting to share with someone
   - ❐ a burden, where I need to talk with someone who knows what it's like
   - ❐ just someone to have fun and celebrate with
   - ❐ someone to share my faith with
   - ❐ other: _____

10. Elizabeth and Mary were obviously close to each other. Louis H. Evans, Jr., in his book *Covenant to Care*, describes eight characteristics of covenant relationships. Many of these characteristics were present in Elizabeth and Mary's relationship. Check the ones that are evident in your closest relationships:

LEADER: When you have completed the Bible Study, move on to the Caring Time (page 37).

- ❏ affirmation: unconditional love
- ❏ availability: all I have is yours
- ❏ prayer: regularly and in crisis
- ❏ openness: share my feelings
- ❏ honesty: speak the truth in love
- ❏ sensitivity: meet you in your need
- ❏ confidentiality: keep your secrets
- ❏ accountability: help each other grow

COMMENT

Elizabeth holds two distinctions in her life. She was the mother of John the Baptist (the forerunner of Jesus), and she was the first to greet Mary as Jesus' mother. Elizabeth was a godly woman. She was the daughter of a family of priests from the house of Aaron, and she was married to a priest. Our passage records that she was a righteous woman, but she was barren.

Imagine the joy and excitement Elizabeth felt when Zechariah came home from the Temple one day and told his wife of the angel's visit and message. She undoubtedly received the message in a spirit of humility and reverent responsibility. She believed strongly in miracles and anxiously awaited the coming of her son. Zechariah's doubts cost him the loss of his voice until after his son was born. Elizabeth knew God's power and did not doubt his ability to allow her to conceive after years of being barren.

When she was six months pregnant, her cousin Mary came for a visit with her own story of an unprecedented and special birth. Imagine the excitement these women must have shared in their common bond of God's favor on their lives. With modesty and a sense of wonder, Elizabeth asks Mary, "But why am I so favored, that the mother of my Lord should come to me?" For three months Elizabeth entertained the mother of the Messiah in her home. Although filled with great dreams and aspirations for her own child, Elizabeth could unselfishly state that Mary's child would be greater than hers. Despite their age difference, they probably shared each other's fears and anticipation at giving birth to such noble men. We wonder if they had any premonition for what would befall their sons in the future. Their shared joy at the birth of their sons would eventually become shared grief at their deaths.

Shortly after Mary's return to her home, Elizabeth gave birth to a son. As was the custom eight days later, they prepared for his circumcision. Even though there were no men named John in the family, Elizabeth proudly declared that this was her son's name. When the family and friends hesitated, Zechariah was asked what his son's name would be. On a tablet, he wrote that his name would be John. Immediately Zechariah's speech returned. The hand of God was with Elizabeth as she shared a special relationship with her husband, her son, and her cousin Mary.

John the Baptist's tribute to Jesus as one mightier than himself and his spirit of renunciation (John 3:30) are reminders of his mother's noble spirit. Elizabeth's lasting memorial as the great mother of John the Baptist is found in the words of Christ when he said, "I tell you the truth: Among those born of women there has not risen anyone greater than John the Baptist" (Matthew 11:11).

 ## CARING TIME / 15–45 Minutes / All Together

Leader: The purpose of the Caring Time in this session is to spend time in caring support for each other through Sharing, Prayer, and Action.

SHARING

Share your response to the following question with your group:

"How can I strengthen my relationship with my spouse,
my best friend, or my children?"

PRAYER

Gather your group in a circle and pray for the concerns and struggles voiced during this meeting. If you want to pray in silence, say the word "Amen" when you finish your prayer, so that the next person will know when to start.

ACTION

Plan two or three concrete steps you can take this week to demonstrate your love for the person(s) you mentioned in the sharing time.

SESSION 5
Pursuing a Life of Service

PURPOSE

To discover what it means to give to others in service to Christ.

AGENDA

 Gathering  Bible Study Caring Time

OPEN

GATHERING / 15 Minutes / All Together
Leader: Read the Instructions for Step One and go first. Then read the Introduction and explain the Bible Study choices.

Step One: MUTUAL FUNDS: You've just been given $10,000 to invest in various mutual funds. How much are you going to invest in each of the following funds?

_____ **Aggressive Christian Growth:** This fund will give great returns to help me grow in my faith. The dividends include a greater love for God and a deeper commitment to my church.

_____ **Fidelity Marriage Fund:** This fund will ensure that my marriage is a wonderful loving relationship. The prospectus promises great communication and a wonderful family life.

_____ **Balanced Time Fund:** This fund will help me to budget my time effectively so my life is balanced. The broker says that this fund a favorite of busy people.

_____ **Conservative Values Fund:** This fund will help my family and friends return to homegrown and traditional lifestyles.

_____ **Friendship Bond Fund:** Closer and deeper friendships is the payoff of this fund. This fund boasts timeless dividends and wealth that "cannot be measured."

_____ **Pacific/Caribbean Restoration Fund:** This fund will take you to exotic places for rest and relaxation. This is a good fund for someone who needs to spend a little on themselves.

_____ **Security Rainy Day Fund:** This mutual fund promises to pay dividends for a rainy day. It is a hedge against any problem or disaster and will keep you from worrying.

_____ **Intelligent Strength Fund:** This is a fund designed for people who need to save money for college. Money invested in this fund will be ready to help a student pay for tuition.

Step Two: PURSUING A LIFE OF SERVICE. Women and service have traditionally gone together. The professions traditionally open to women—teaching, nursing, and secretarial work—are service-oriented professions. In addition, a woman's role in marriage has been seen as serving her husband. Often, these roles do not carry with them much respect or honor. As Aretha Franklin sings, we want a little R-E-S-P-E-C-T! Many women today are rediscovering a biblical model of service. This model stresses service that is given to God and to others in his name. Without service, we can never be obedient to Christ or live a full and meaningful life.

"There is no higher religion than human service. To work for the common good is the greatest creed."
—Albert Schweitzer

Service can take on many different forms. Certainly what we do for our friends and family is a part of service. The work we do in our church and community is another part as well. We know the importance of charitable work (the work we do for no human reward or payment). When we have done a good deed, there is a feeling within our hearts that cannot be duplicated by money or other compensation.

More and more demands are made on our time, including demands from family, friends, work, career, children, and continuing education. You may wonder: where on earth can I find time to do things for others? It's a difficult balancing act. But we are called as people of faith to give ourselves in service to others. In the words of Christ, "if you have done it to the least of these my brethren you have done it unto me."

LEADER: Choose the OPTION 1 Bible Study (below) or the OPTION 2 Study (page 43).

In Option One, we will consider the example of the Shunammite woman who opened her home to the prophet Elisha (from the second book of Kings). In our Option Two Study (from the book of Acts), we will consider the life of Dorcas, a woman who was known for her acts of charity.

BIBLE STUDY / 30 Minutes / Groups of 4

Leader: Help the group choose an Option for study. Divide into groups of 4 for discussion. Remind the Convener for each foursome to move the group along so the Bible Study can be completed in the time allotted. Ask everyone to return together for the Caring Time for the final 15–45 minutes.

OPTION 1

Old Testament Study / Shunammite Woman
2 Kings 4:8–17

STUDY

The following passage describes an encounter of a woman who was open to God's direction as she helped the prophet Elisha. Read 2 Kings 4:8–17 and the Comment section (page 42). Then discuss the questions which follow with your group.

⁸One day Elisha went to Shunem. And a well-to-do woman was there, who urged him to stay for a meal. So whenever he came by, he stopped there to eat. ⁹She said to her husband, "I know that this man who often comes our way is a holy man of God. ¹⁰Let's make a small room on the roof and put in it a bed and a table, a chair and a lamp for him. Then he can stay there whenever he comes to us."

¹¹One day when Elisha came, he went up to his room and lay down there. ¹²He said to his servant Gehazi, "Call the Shunammite." So he called her, and she stood before him. ¹³Elisha said to him, "Tell her, 'You have gone to all this trouble for us. Now what can be done for you? Can we speak on your behalf to the king or the commander of the army?' "

She replied, "I have a home among my own people."

¹⁴"What can be done for her?" Elisha asked.

Gehazi said, "Well, she has no son and her husband is old."

¹⁵Then Elisha said, "Call her." So he called her, and she stood in the doorway. ¹⁶"About this time next year," Elisha said, "you will hold a son in your arms."

"No, my lord," she objected. "Don't mislead your servant, O man of God!"

¹⁷But the woman became pregnant, and the next year about that same time she gave birth to a son, just as Elisha had told her.

2 Kings 4:8–17, NIV

1. What seems strange to you in this story?
   - ❏ that a wealthy person would help a prophet
   - ❏ that the woman could convince her husband to make a room for a stranger
   - ❏ that Elisha would promise this woman a son
   - ❏ that Elisha's servant Gehazi does all Elisha's talking for him

2. Which of the following words best describes this Shunammite woman as you meet her in this story?
   - ❏ naive
   - ❏ thoughtful
   - ❏ humble
   - ❏ trusting
   - ❏ manipulative
   - ❏ perceptive
   - ❏ foolhardy
   - ❏ religious
   - ❏ self-sacrificing
   - ❏ other: _____

3. Have you ever had a friendship with a man that others didn't quite understand? That even you didn't understand?

4. What is the woman feeling in verse 16?
   - ❑ She lacks faith.
   - ❑ She is cautiously optimistic.
   - ❑ She is realistically hopeful.
   - ❑ She is afraid to hope for a child.
   - ❑ She is frightened—how could Elisha know this about her?
   - ❑ She is confused.
   - ❑ She is afraid to die.

5. This woman evidently had the gift of hospitality, as she opened her home to Elisha. What gifts has God given you? How are you using them to serve him?

6. What was the attitude toward strangers in your home as a child?
   - ❑ There are no strangers here—only friends we haven't met.
   - ❑ Do not forget to entertain strangers, for by so doing some people have entertained angels without knowing it (Heb. 13:2).
   - ❑ Don't talk to strangers!
   - ❑ Show kindness to "people like us"; with others, beware!
   - ❑ With strangers, "be as shrewd as snakes and as innocent as doves" (Matthew 10:16).

7. Finish this sentence: "A woman who serves others like this ..."
   - ❑ should get a life.
   - ❑ has low self-esteem.
   - ❑ has a naturally generous spirit.
   - ❑ is generally after something in return.
   - ❑ has discovered the true meaning of life.
   - ❑ other: _____

8. When was the last time you went out of your way to provide for someone else, as the Shunammite woman did? How did you feel about what you did?

9. What is the most important reward you look for from serving someone else?
   - ❑ something they do in return for me
   - ❑ the good feeling I get from helping
   - ❑ their thanks
   - ❑ their friendship
   - ❑ the knowledge that I have pleased God
   - ❑ other: _____

10. Finish this sentence: "I would serve others more if ..."
- ❏ I knew I would be rewarded.
- ❏ I didn't have so many troubles of my own.
- ❏ I had more time.
- ❏ I weren't so wrapped up in myself.
- ❏ God would show me the best way for me to get involved.
- ❏ other: _____

11. What do you need to do in response to this session?
- ❏ open myself to God's leading about where I could serve others
- ❏ re-order my time priorities
- ❏ keep on doing what I am doing
- ❏ nothing—I need to focus on getting my own life together.
- ❏ stop being so focused on myself

LEADER: When you have finished the Bible Study, move on to the Caring Time (page 45).

COMMENT

In the King James Version, this woman is called "great" (2 Kings 4:8). This probably means that she was a wealthy and influential woman and a leader in her community. But her story shows that she was great in other ways as well—in her faith, wisdom, silence, and her service to the rich and poor alike. Little is said about her husband. But he is probably older than she is, and he evidently trusts his wife's judgment.

She started by preparing some bread for Elisha when she heard he was passing through town. This relationship deepened over time: Elisha was invited to stay overnight, and was eventually given a room which was furnished with "all the comforts of home." In return for her kindness, Elisha promises her a son by the next year. She had probably been barren so long that she couldn't even think about having a child. But how overjoyed she must have been when her son arrived!

But when the child was an early adolescent, he became deathly sick with a heat stroke and died. The woman calmly laid her son on the prophet's bed and went to seek out Elisha. First his servant, Gehazi, tried to revive the boy to no avail. Finally, Elisha arrived. He stretched his body over the boy's, and breathed life into him again.

Years later when a famine was approaching, Elisha warned the woman to take her son and escape to the land of the Philistines, which she did. They returned seven years later only to find that their home had been confiscated by King Jehoram. She kept her silence until she could appeal directly to the King. When she had an audience with the King, there stood Gehazi speaking on her behalf. The King was so moved by her story that he made sure that her home was restored to her and to her son.

New Testament Study / Dorcas
Acts 9:36–42

STUDY

Dorcas gave so generously of herself to others that even today her name is synonymous with acts of charity. The motivating principle in Dorcas' life is given in these words from Acts 9:36, "who was always doing good and helping the poor." Using a sewing needle as her tool and her home as her workshop, she helped many others. She was probably a woman who was somewhat wealthy. While she could have easily given money, she chose to give herself in service to the needs of others. Read Acts 9:36–43 and discuss the questions which follow with your group.

³⁶In Joppa there was a disciple named Tabitha (which, when translated, is Dorcas), who was always doing good and helping the poor. ³⁷About that time she became sick and died, and her body was washed and placed in an upstairs room. ³⁸Lydda was near Joppa; so when the disciples heard that Peter was in Lydda, they sent two men to him and urged him, "Please come at once!"

³⁹Peter went with them, and when he arrived he was taken upstairs to the room. All the widows stood around him, crying and showing him the robes and other clothing that Dorcas had made while she was still with them.

⁴⁰Peter sent them all out of the room; then he got down on his knees and prayed. Turning toward the dead woman, he said, "Tabitha, get up." She opened her eyes, and seeing Peter she sat up. ⁴¹He took her by the hand and helped her to her feet. Then he called the believers and the widows and presented her to them alive. ⁴²This became known all over Joppa, and many people believed in the Lord.

Acts 9:36–42, NIV

"I will not just live my life, I will not just spend my life. I will invest my life."
—Helen Keller

1. If you were a reporter for The Joppa Journal and you were assigned to do a story on this event, who would you want to interview first?
   - ❏ Tabitha, to find out what it was like to be dead
   - ❏ Peter, to find out how he did this
   - ❏ the crying widows, to find out what sort of person Tabitha was
   - ❏ a local physician, to get a medical opinion

2. Why do you suppose the widows thought it was important to show the clothing that Dorcas (Tabitha) had made?
   - ❏ Little reminders like that really get to you when you're mourning.
   - ❏ They wanted Peter to see how talented she was so he would do a miracle for her.
   - ❏ They were upset because they had lost their seamstress.
   - ❏ The woman's love was expressed in her work.
   - ❏ other: _____

3. What good deeds did you do as a child?
- ❐ helped a neighbor with some chores
- ❐ helped my parents around the house
- ❐ helped my parents care for an ailing relative
- ❐ helped with the needy in my church
- ❐ other: _____

4. As a child, how did you feel about doing those good deeds? I felt:
- ❐ I was making a difference.
- ❐ I wasn't really making a difference.
- ❐ I was doing it because I had to.
- ❐ guilty that I wasn't doing more.
- ❐ proud that I was doing something.
- ❐ I didn't really think about it.
- ❐ other: _____

"Love is always open arms. If you close your arms about love you will find that you are left holding only yourself."
—Leo Buscaglia

5. Dorcas made things by hand for people she cared about. What hand-made things do you remember receiving as a child?

6. How did you feel about receiving these handmade things?
- ❐ honored and special
- ❐ cheated—I figured people made things because it was cheaper.
- ❐ I didn't know the difference—it was all the same to me.
- ❐ I thought it was what everyone got.
- ❐ other: _____

7. What do you think motivated Dorcas to do her acts of charity?
- ❐ her love for God
- ❐ her desire to have a good reputation
- ❐ her desire to have people speak well of her
- ❐ her devotion to the Christian life
- ❐ other: _____

8. What motivates you to do acts of charity?
- ❐ my view of Scripture
- ❐ my view of the role of women in the church
- ❐ my view of social responsibility
- ❐ my upbringing
- ❐ the tax deduction
- ❐ guilt
- ❐ other: _____

LEADER: When you have completed the Bible Study, move on to the Caring Time (below).

9. What prevents you from doing additional acts of charity?
   ❑ lack of time
   ❑ lack of money
   ❑ overwhelmed by the need
   ❑ other responsibilities
   ❑ other: _____

10. If you were to die, what could people show to a "Peter" to indicate how much you cared for them?

CARING TIME / 15–45 Minutes / All Together
Leader: Bring all of the foursomes back together for a time of caring. Follow the three steps below.

SHARING

Share with your group a specific prayer concern you have about your acts of service.

PRAYER

Remembering the requests that were just shared, close with a prayer time. The Leader can start a conversational prayer (short phrases and sentences in the style of a normal conversation), with group members following as they wish. After an appropriate amount of time, the Leader can close by praying for requests not already mentioned.

ACTION

Identify two servant tasks you can do in your community. Make plans to do them this week.

SESSION 6
Pursuing a Life of Faith

PURPOSE To discover ways to strengthen my faith in God.

AGENDA  Gathering  Bible Study  Caring Time

OPEN   ## GATHERING / 15 Minutes / All Together
Leader: Read the instructions for Step One and go first. Then read the Introduction and explain the choices for Bible Study.

Step One: CHRISTIAN BASICS. How do you view the Christian faith? Answer these questions about different topics and freely discuss your answers with the group. Remember that there are no right or wrong answers.

1. This is what I think about prayer:
   - ❐ wishful thinking
   - ❐ direct line to God
   - ❐ magic
   - ❐ a life saver
   - ❐ a psychological exercise
   - ❐ powerful
   - ❐ a daily practice
   - ❐ positive thinking

2. This is what I think about church:
   - ❐ boring
   - ❐ friendly
   - ❐ fun
   - ❐ It doesn't meet my needs.
   - ❐ too traditional
   - ❐ inspiring
   - ❐ always asking for money
   - ❐ confusing—too many types

3. This is what I think about the Bible:
   - ❐ hard to read
   - ❐ inspiring
   - ❐ hard to apply
   - ❐ full of violence
   - ❐ outdated
   - ❐ full of promises
   - ❐ secret to life
   - ❐ I need help interpreting it.

4. This is what I think about Christians:
   - ❐ more loving
   - ❐ too conservative
   - ❐ world changers
   - ❐ too extreme
   - ❐ hypocrites
   - ❐ too liberal
   - ❐ God's people
   - ❐ just like everyone else

Step Two: PURSUING A LIFE OF FAITH. The most important part of our lives which we can pursue is our life of faith. As Scripture records, "What good will it be for a man (or a woman) if he (she) gains the whole world, yet forfeits his (her) soul?" (Matthew 16:36). We may know that our faith is the most important part of our lives, and we may even verbalize that belief. But do our lives reflect this?

Living a life of faith does not mean that we never encounter trials and hardships. But our faith affects our response to those trials and hardships. No one is immune from life's tragedies. However, Christians can rely on their faith in God and in his sovereign power to take care of them and to see them through the difficult times. How do we handle the times when we cannot sense God's presence and we feel that he has abandoned us? How do we express our faith in God's power in our lives? Those are some of the questions we will address in this session.

LEADER:
Choose the
OPTION 1 Bible
Study (below)
or the OPTION 2
Study (page 51).

In Option One (from the book of Genesis), we will consider the life of Sarah, the wife of Abraham. They are a prime example of a couple who lived by faith, but still at times had doubts. In Option Two (from John's Gospel), we will consider the life of Mary, the mother of Jesus, for she too exemplified a life of faith.

BIBLE STUDY / 30 Minutes / Groups of 4

Leader: Help the group choose an Option for study. Divide into groups of 4 for discussion. Remind the Convener for each foursome to move the group along so the Bible Study can be completed in the time allotted. Ask everyone to return together for the Caring Time for the final 15–45 minutes.

OPTION 1

Old Testament Study / Sarah
Genesis 18:1–2, 9–15; 21:1–7

STUDY

In her old age, Sarah is told that she will have a child. Although she disbelieves the news at first, she later becomes a model of faith and devotion to God. Read Genesis 18:1–2, 9–15; 21:1–7 and discuss your responses to the following questions with the group.

18 *The LORD appeared to Abraham near the great trees of Mamre while he was sitting at the entrance to his tent in the heat of the day.* *²Abraham looked up and saw three men standing nearby. When he saw them, he hurried from the entrance of his tent to meet them and bowed low to the ground. ...*

⁹*"Where is your wife Sarah?" they asked him.*

"There, in the tent," he said.

¹⁰*Then the LORD said, "I will surely return to you about this time next year, and Sarah your wife will have a son."*

Now Sarah was listening at the entrance to the tent, which was behind him. ¹¹*Abraham and Sarah were already old and well advanced in years, and Sarah was past the age of childbearing.* ¹²*So Sarah laughed to herself as she thought, "After I am worn out and my master is old, will I now have this pleasure?"*

¹³*Then the LORD said to Abraham, "Why did Sarah laugh and say, 'Will I really have a child, now that I am old?' ¹⁴Is anything too hard for the LORD? I will return to you at the appointed time next year and Sarah will have a son."*

¹⁵*Sarah was afraid, so she lied and said, "I did not laugh."*

But he said, "Yes, you did laugh." ...

21 *Now the LORD was gracious to Sarah as he had said, and the LORD did for Sarah what he had promised.* ²*Sarah became pregnant and bore a son to Abraham in his old age, at the very time God had promised him.* ³*Abraham gave the name Isaac to the son Sarah bore him.* ⁴*When his son Isaac was eight days old, Abraham circumcised him, as God commanded him.* ⁵*Abraham was a hundred years old when his son Isaac was born to him.*

⁶*Sarah said, "God has brought me laughter, and everyone who hears about this will laugh with me." ⁷And she added, "Who would have said to Abraham that Sarah would nurse children? Yet I have borne him a son in his old age."*

Genesis 18:1–2, 9–15; 21:1–7, NIV

1. What is your initial reaction to these passages about Sarah?
   - ❏ It sounds as if she doubted as much as she had faith.
   - ❏ You'd think she wouldn't have doubted when God spoke to her husband directly.
   - ❏ Why didn't God speak to Sarah directly?
   - ❏ I wish God would give me my heart's desire.
   - ❏ Sounds like folklore—normal acts magnified by time.
   - ❏ We need to tell the stories of people like this who are living today.

2. Write your own definition of faith (see Hebrews 11:1):

   "Faith is ..."

"A faith that hasn't been tested can't be trusted."
—Adrian Rogers

48

3. In childhood, who served as an example of faith to you?
- ❐ my father
- ❐ my mother
- ❐ a grandparent
- ❐ a pastor
- ❐ a Sunday school teacher
- ❐ a youth group adviser
- ❐ an adult friend
- ❐ other: _____

4. What is the purpose of your faith?
- ❐ to get what I want from God
- ❐ to fulfill all of my dreams
- ❐ to encourage others in the faith
- ❐ to glorify God
- ❐ to make me a stronger Christian
- ❐ I don't think my faith has a purpose.
- ❐ other: _____

5. Why did Sarah laugh when she overheard the visitors?
- ❐ because she knew they didn't know how old she was
- ❐ because she couldn't imagine giving birth at her age
- ❐ because she doubted God
- ❐ because she remembered a good joke she had heard
- ❐ because she loved Abraham being caught in this situation
- ❐ other: _____

6. How would you describe Sarah's laughter?
- ❐ situational—You really had to be there.
- ❐ suppressed—She was trying to contain herself.
- ❐ sarcastic—"Yeah, and Abraham will run the marathon."
- ❐ sinful—She displayed her lack of faith.
- ❐ spiritual—She was honest with her feelings.

7. What do you need to laugh about right now?
- ❐ my relationships with men
- ❐ the stress in my career
- ❐ the stress in my family life
- ❐ my own shortcomings
- ❐ my financial worries
- ❐ my mortality
- ❐ other: _____

8. In what ways has God "brought you laughter" as he did to Sarah?
- ❐ through my children
- ❐ through my husband (or significant other)
- ❐ through friends who were with me in difficult times
- ❐ through helping me to see the humor myself in stressful situations
- ❐ through all of the joys he has placed in my life

9. Undoubtedly, Sarah had given up her desire to have a son. Where in your life have you given up on your dream?

☐ in my quest for romance
☐ in my quest for vocational fulfillment
☐ in my quest for spiritual understanding
☐ in my quest for self-understanding
☐ in my quest to accomplish something significant with my life
☐ in my desire for a family
☐ other: _____

LEADER: When
you have com-
pleted the Bible
Study, move on
to the Caring
Time (page 54).

10. Where in your life is God telling you that "it is never too late"?

11. Sarah had to wait over 20 years to see God's promise come true in her life. How patient are you with God's promises? Put an "✗" on the line below:

_____

not at all   moderately   I'm a model
                                                            of patience

COMMENT

Sarah's life was one continuous trial of her faith in God's promise that she would be the Mother of Nations. Edith Deen writes, "Through her life of trials she emerged as a woman of power, one who was dutiful and beloved wife and who finally became a favored and venerated mother."

During the time of history when Sarah lived (probably around the 19th or 20th century B.C.), a woman was not important until she had given her husband a son. The father and the family line could only live on through the son. The tragedy of Sarah's early life was that she was barren. However, the miracle of her life was that she eventually gave birth to Isaac ("Son of Promise") when (from our point of view) her biological clock had run out of time.

Sarah accompanied her husband on their nomadic wanderings, not as his shadow, but as a strong influence. Sarah shared her husband's dangers and heartaches, as well as his dreams. Sarah remained faithful to her husband and to God in the bad times as well as in the good times. Eleven years after leaving their homeland (and first receiving the promise of their having a son), Sarah concludes that she is the problem. With wavering faith, but also a willingness to forsake her own vanity, she gives her handmaiden Hagar to Abraham (Genesis 16:2). Hagar bears him a son, Ishmael. Sarah's lack of faith in her ability to give birth to her own child was to bring her years of anguish. For she would later learn that this was not the child that God had promised. Thirteen years after Ishmael was born, God reminds them that Sarah will still bear the child of promise.

When Isaac approached manhood, Sarah endured her greatest trial yet. At God's command, Abraham took his son Isaac on a long journey up the side of the mountain to sacrifice him to God. We can imagine the anguish in Sarah's heart as she watched her husband and beloved son depart for the land of Moriah. But still this woman, who had developed a great faith, could turn to the omnipotent God, who had miraculously given her this child in her old age. She remained obedient to this God of love and mercy. And soon she discovered that God had provided another sacrifice.

There is no further record of Sarah after Isaac's return from Moriah. But we can imagine that she shared and enjoyed the love of her devoted husband and son until she died at the age of 127 years. She is the only woman in the Bible whose age is recorded at her death—a further indication of her importance to the Hebrew people.

OPTION 2

New Testament Study / Mary, Mother of Jesus
John 2:1–11

STUDY

In this section of John's Gospel, Jesus moves from the end of his private life to the beginning of his public ministry. His mother Mary plays a significant role in this transitional period. Read John 2:1–11 and discuss your responses to the following questions with your group.

2 *On the third day a wedding took place at Cana in Galilee. Jesus' mother was there, [2]and Jesus and his disciples had also been invited to the wedding. [3]When the wine was gone, Jesus' mother said to him, "They have no more wine."*

[4]"Dear woman, why do you involve me?" Jesus replied. "My time has not yet come."

[5]His mother said to the servants, "Do whatever he tells you."

[6]Nearby stood six stone water jars, the kind used by the Jews for ceremonial washing, each holding from twenty to thirty gallons.

[7]Jesus said to the servants, "Fill the jars with water"; so they filled them to the brim.

[8]Then he told them, "Now draw some out and take it to the master of the banquet."

They did so, [9]and the master of the banquet tasted the water that had been turned into wine. He did not realize where it had come from, though the servants who had drawn the water knew. Then he called the bridegroom aside [10]and said, "Everyone brings out the choice wine first and then the cheaper wine after the guests have had too much to drink; but you have saved the best till now."

[11]This, the first of his miraculous signs, Jesus performed at Cana in Galilee. He thus revealed his glory, and his disciples put their faith in him.

John 2:1–11, NIV

1. Imagine that you were a reporter for *The Cana Courier*. What headline would you give this news story?
   ❏ "Local Wedding Turns into Wine Tasting Party"
   ❏ "Mother Watches Son Perform Miracle"
   ❏ "Local Man Changes Water into Wine at Wedding"
   ❏ "Magical Miracle Makes Merriment Merrier"

2. Jesus hadn't performed any miracles yet. When they ran out of wine, why did Mary approach him?
   ❏ out of concern for the guests
   ❏ to get the bridegroom out of a jam
   ❏ She was catering the party.
   ❏ She had faith that Jesus could do something.

3. If you could choose any miracle to start off your new job (or ministry), what would it be?
   ❏ healing the multitudes
   ❏ negotiating a peace treaty between warring nations
   ❏ paying off the national debt in one day
   ❏ averting a natural disaster
   ❏ leading a national revival
   ❏ creating the winning lottery ticket
   ❏ other: _____

4. What is the significance of Mary's words to the servants in verse 5?
   ❏ It shows her faith in her son.
   ❏ She knew Jesus would come through.
   ❏ She didn't know what else to say.
   ❏ She hoped that she could pressure Jesus into doing something.

5. How do you think Jesus felt when Mary asked him to do something?
   ❏ upset   ❏ annoyed
   ❏ embarrassed   ❏ reluctant
   ❏ willing   ❏ other: _____

6. When you were an adolescent, how often did your mother pressure you to do something you didn't want to do?
   ❏ She had developed it into an art form.
   ❏ She did it, but later I understood it was for my own good.
   ❏ She did it, but I never saw the good in it.
   ❏ She rarely did that.
   ❏ She *still* does that!

"Faith can put a candle in the darkest night."
—Margaret Sangster

7. Where do you need to see the "water turned into wine" in your life?
   - ❒ self esteem: feeling blah, worthless, useless, and out of it
   - ❒ family: feeling hassled, haggard, strung out, and put through the wringer
   - ❒ work/school: feeling pushed, pressed, and overloaded
   - ❒ appearance: feeling unattractive
   - ❒ spiritual life: feeling lonely, dry, and out of synch with God
   - ❒ physical life: feeling worn out, used up, drained
   - ❒ mental life: feeling dumb, stupid, like my brain has taken a vacation

8. How would you describe the situation you checked in question #7, in terms of this Scripture?
   - ❒ The wine has run out completely.
   - ❒ There's new wine available, but I'm not drinking.
   - ❒ I've tried the new wine but nothing has changed.
   - ❒ I'm not sure that the new wine is any better.
   - ❒ I'm waiting for my "Mary" to ask God to do something for me.
   - ❒ I'm sipping, but not drinking deeply.
   - ❒ other: _____

LEADER: When you have completed the Bible Study, move on to the Caring Time (page 54).

9. If you had Jesus by your side, how would you ask him to intervene for you in this situation?

COMMENT

Mary lived a life of faith. There were times when she didn't understand what God was doing in her life, but she continued to trust him. Her heart was always open to God's direction and leading. Her divine mission of being the mother of God's son never wavered from the manger to Calvary. She displayed great wisdom and spiritual discernment in her son's circumcision, presentation at the Temple, and in her own appearance at the Temple for purification rites (40 days after Jesus' birth). She trusted God when they fled to Egypt (because of Herod's threats).

Mary was reminded of her son's special place in history when he was 12 years old and they left him at the Temple. When they caught up with him, Jesus said that he had to be doing his Father's work. She took what he said and "pondered these things in her heart" (Luke 2:51). Perhaps Mary remembered those words at the wedding feast at Cana. Although she didn't fully understand her son's mission in life, she had faith in God that her son was special. So she instructed the servants to do whatever Jesus told them to do. This was her son's farewell to private life and the beginning of his public ministry. His words to her (John 2:4) must have tried her faith, but she remained patient and trusting.

Even at the foot of the cross, Mary may not have fully understood the reason why her son had to die—let alone be crucified. But she continued to trust. And after her time of private grieving, she assisted the disciples in carrying out her son's ministry. Her knowledge of God and his promises to her sustained her. Although we do not know how Mary felt upon hearing that her son was raised from the dead, we do know that her ministry continued. In Acts, it is recorded that she was gathered with the early church after the Ascension (Acts 1:14).

 CARING TIME / 15–45 Minutes / All Together

Leader: Bring all of the foursomes back together for a time of Caring. Follow the three steps below.

SHARING | What challenge in your personal life (in respect to your faith) do you think you will face this week that you would like prayer for? Share this with the group.

PRAYER | If someone is still uncomfortable praying aloud, encourage them to pray silently. When they conclude their prayer, ask them to say "Amen" so the next person will know to continue.

ACTION | Choose one area of your life where you want to exercise more faith. Plan one or two concrete things you can do this week to increase your faith.

SESSION 7
Pursuing Our Potential

PURPOSE

To discover ways to realize our fullest potential as women who are created in the image of God.

AGENDA

 Gathering  **Bible Study**  **Caring Time**

OPEN

 ## GATHERING / 15 Minutes / All Together

Leader: This is the final session together. You may want to have your Caring Time first. If not, be sure to allow a full 25 minutes at the end of the session.

Step One: YOU REMIND ME OF... Write down the initials of the person from your small group who reminds you of the following national parks. Share your responses with the group.

____ **Grand Canyon National Park:** What an impressive vista! You have character that has taken years of effort and constant attention.

____ **Statue of Liberty National Monument:** You are a living symbol to those around you of freedom, hope, and new life.

____ **Golden Gate National Park:** You bring people together and bridge the gap in a beautiful, stunning way.

____ **Mount Rushmore:** You are an enduring testimony to leadership, character, and integrity.

____ **Sequoia National Park:** Your growth is so impressive that you reach into the skies and provide shade and security for many creatures.

____ **Yellowstone National Park:** With your hot springs and geysers, you are a source of warmth for those who get close to you.

____ **Yosemite National Park:** You are the most popular choice for an exciting and adventurous experience!

____ **Mount Rainier National Park:** You keep people looking up, and your high standards can be seen from a great distance.

____ **The Alamo:** You remind everyone who sees you of courage, tenacity, and determination.

Step Two: PURSUING OUR POTENTIAL. Now we reach the culmination of our sessions together. How do we take all that we have studied and learned and use it to reach our potential? As we mentioned in the first session, it is a juggling act. It's hard to keep every aspect of our lives in balance. What is the end result of all our hard work and pursuits? Is the desired result to be more knowledgeable, to be whole, to have healthier relationships, to live a life of service, and to live a life of faith? The answer is "yes" and "no." "Yes," because we do want to pursue all these noble attributes. But also "no," because our goal in life should not be to attain these attributes simply in order to be a better person. The first question in the Westminster Catechism is "What is the chief end of man (and woman)?" The answer is: "To glorify God and to enjoy him forever."

Everything we do and achieve in our lives should help us to realize our potential as women who are created in the image of God. Only when we do these things do we realize our full potential and become the women of God that he wants us to be. We have a responsibility to be all that we can be for God's glory, not our own.

LEADER:
Choose the
OPTION 1 Bible
Study (below)
or the OPTION 2
Study (page 60).

In the Option One Study (from the Book of Judges), we will learn about the first female political leader of the Israelites. That's right—a housewife who realizes her potential and heeds God's call to lead his people. In the Option Two Study (from the Acts of the Apostles), we will study the life of Priscilla (one of the early church leaders)—a woman who worked alongside her husband in the church.

BIBLE STUDY / 25 Minutes / Groups of 4
Leader: Remind the Conveners to end their Bible Study time 5 minutes earlier than usual to allow ample time for your final Caring Time—deciding what the group will do next.

OPTION 1

Old Testament Study / Deborah
Judges 4:1–16

STUDY

Deborah is the only woman mentioned in the Bible who was placed at the height of political power by the common consent of the people. She lived in the time of the Judges, approximately 13 centuries before Christ. Few women in all of history have attained the public dignity and supreme authority of Deborah. Read Judges 4:1–16 and discuss your responses to the following questions with your group.

4 After Ehud died, the Israelites once again did evil in the eyes of the LORD. ²So the LORD sold them into the hands of Jabin, a king of Canaan, who reigned in Hazor. The commander of his army was Sisera, who lived in Harosheth Haggoyim. ³Because he had nine hundred iron chariots and had cruelly oppressed the Israelites for twenty years, they cried to the LORD for help.

⁴Deborah, a prophetess, the wife of Lappidoth, was leading Israel at that time. ⁵She held court under the Palm of Deborah between Ramah and Bethel in the hill country of Ephraim, and the Israelites came to her to have their disputes decided. ⁶She sent for Barak son of Abinoam from Kedesh in Naphtali and said to him, "The LORD, the God of Israel, commands you: 'Go, take with you ten thousand men of Naphtali and Zebulun and lead the way to Mount Tabor. ⁷I will lure Sisera, the commander of Jabin's army, with his chariots and his troops to the Kishon River and give him into your hands.' "

⁸Barak said to her, "If you go with me, I will go; but if you don't go with me, I won't go."

⁹"Very well," Deborah said, "I will go with you. But because of the way you are going about this, the honor will not be yours, for the LORD will hand Sisera over to a woman." So Deborah went with Barak to Kedesh, ¹⁰where he summoned Zebulun and Naphtali. Ten thousand men followed him, and Deborah also went with him.

¹¹Now Heber the Kenite had left the other Kenites, the descendants of Hobab, Moses' brother-in-law, and pitched his tent by the great tree in Zaanannim near Kedesh.

¹²When they told Sisera that Barak son of Abinoam had gone up to Mount Tabor, ¹³Sisera gathered together his nine hundred iron chariots and all the men with him, from Harosheth Haggoyim to the Kishon River.

¹⁴Then Deborah said to Barak, "Go! This is the day the LORD has given Sisera into your hands. Has not the LORD gone ahead of you?" So Barak went down Mount Tabor, followed by ten thousand men. ¹⁵At Barak's advance, the LORD routed Sisera and all his chariots and army by the sword, and Sisera abandoned his chariot and fled on foot. ¹⁶But Barak pursued the chariots and army as far as Harosheth Haggoyim. All the troops of Sisera fell by the sword; not a man was left.

Judges 4:1–16, NIV

1. What is your initial reaction to this passage?
   ❑ I never knew this passage existed.
   ❑ I can't believe the Israelites had a woman leader.
   ❑ This must be a typo.
   ❑ If you want a job done well, give it to a woman.

2. What was the most important qualification Deborah had that God needed in a leader?
   - ❑ She could speak for God. (prophet)
   - ❑ She was wise in her ability to mediate disputes. (judge)
   - ❑ She was courageous.
   - ❑ She was a gifted military strategist.
   - ❑ She had faith in God.

3. Which courageous woman (real or fictitious) did you admire in your childhood or adolescence?
   - ❑ Eleanor Roosevelt
   - ❑ Wonder Woman
   - ❑ Mother Teresa
   - ❑ Joni Eareckson Tada
   - ❑ Princess Leia (Star Wars)
   - ❑ Betty Ford
   - ❑ Coretta Scott King
   - ❑ Amelia Earhart
   - ❑ Joan of Arc
   - ❑ other: _____

4. On the following women's issues, put an "**X**" on the scale according to which position is closest to yours:

ABILITIES:

women are the inferior sex	women are the superior sex

LEADERSHIP:

women are the inferior sex	women are the superior sex

ROLES:

women are the inferior sex	women are the superior sex

AUTHORITY:

women are the inferior sex	women are the superior sex

5. Why do you think Barak refused to go into battle without Deborah?
   - ❑ He was chicken.
   - ❑ He wasn't sure of the route.
   - ❑ He wasn't convinced that this was the right thing to do.
   - ❑ He needed a spokesperson for God with him.
   - ❑ He saw a spiritual strength in her that he needed.

"Bad will be the day for every man when he becomes absolutely content with the life that he is living, with the thoughts that he is thinking, with the deeds that he is doing, when there is not forever beating at the doors of his soul some great desire to do something larger, which he knows that he was meant and made to do because he is still, in spite of all, the child of God."
—Phillips Brooks

58

"Do not let what you cannot do interfere with what you can do."
—John Wooden

6. If you had Deborah's confidence, what would you attempt?
   - ❐ to tell off my boss
   - ❐ to start on a new career
   - ❐ to seek a position of leadership in my church or community
   - ❐ to go into business for myself
   - ❐ to assert myself more in a conflict I'm in
   - ❐ to develop a creative talent that I think I have
   - ❐ other: _____

7. What is keeping you from realizing your potential?
   - ❐ money
   - ❐ my family
   - ❐ self-confidence
   - ❐ fears
   - ❐ time
   - ❐ lack of motivation
   - ❐ my present job
   - ❐ other: _____
   - ❐ I am realizing my potential.

LEADER: When you have completed the Bible Study, move on to the Caring Time (page 62).

8. What have people told you over the years which has helped or inhibited you from reaching your potential?

9. Where in your life do you wish you possessed Deborah's certainty and confidence?

COMMENT

Deborah was the wife of an obscure gentleman named Lapidoth. The rabbis reported that she was the keeper of the lamps in the tabernacle. Later she would be the keeper of a new vision for the nation of Israel. Deborah fulfilled her potential through three main roles: she was a counselor to the people, a judge in their disputes, and a deliverer in a time of war. She rose in leadership because of her obvious faith and trust in God, and she inspired that same trust in others.

While the people she served lived in fear of the enemy, Deborah's heart burned with indignation at the oppression of her people. As Edith Deen writes, "A gifted and intrepid woman, she felt a call to rise up against such fear and complacency, for she carried in her heart the great hope that God would come to her people's rescue if they would honor Him." Because the men of Israel had faltered in their leadership, Deborah arose to denounce this lack of leadership. She also declared deliverance from the present oppression. She had a great religious zeal and patriotic fervor. As she counseled with her people, she began to see their common danger, and "she kindled in them an enthusiasm for immediate action against the enemy" (Deen).

Against the odds, victory was theirs that day. Deborah took no credit for herself, but gave all the glory to God. To celebrate this great victory, the Ode of Deborah (one of the earliest martial songs in history) was composed (Judges 5). This ordinary woman was able to do extraordinary things for her people because she realized her potential in God's eyes.

OPTION 2

New Testament Study / Priscilla
Acts 18:18–28

STUDY

Priscilla was one of the most influential women in the New Testament church. Read Acts 18:18–28 and discuss your responses to the following questions with your group.

18Paul stayed on in Corinth for some time. Then he left the brothers and sailed for Syria, accompanied by Priscilla and Aquila. Before he sailed, he had his hair cut off at Cenchrea because of a vow he had taken. 19They arrived at Ephesus, where Paul left Priscilla and Aquila. He himself went into the synagogue and reasoned with the Jews. 20When they asked him to spend more time with them, he declined. 21But as he left, he promised, "I will come back if it is God's will." Then he set sail from Ephesus. 22When he landed at Caesarea, he went up and greeted the church and then went down to Antioch.

23After spending some time in Antioch, Paul set out from there and traveled from place to place throughout the region of Galatia and Phrygia, strengthening all the disciples.

24Meanwhile a Jew named Apollos, a native of Alexandria, came to Ephesus. He was a learned man, with a thorough knowledge of the Scriptures. 25He had been instructed in the way of the Lord, and he spoke with great fervor and taught about Jesus accurately, though he knew only the baptism of John. 26He began to speak boldly in the synagogue. When Priscilla and Aquila heard him, they invited him to their home and explained to him the way of God more adequately.

27When Apollos wanted to go to Achaia, the brothers encouraged him and wrote to the disciples there to welcome him. On arriving, he was a great help to those who by grace had believed. 28For he vigorously refuted the Jews in public debate, proving from the Scriptures that Jesus was the Christ.

Acts 18:18–28, NIV

1. What surprises you the most in this passage?
   - ❏ that Paul cut his hair off for a vow
   - ❏ that Priscilla's name is mentioned ahead of her husband's
   - ❏ that an educated Christian like Apollos would not understand something as basic as baptism
   - ❏ that an educated Christian man like Apollos would accept instruction from a woman

2. Priscilla was a great help to Apollos as she taught him the basics of the Christian faith. Who was very helpful to you when you were young in the faith?

3. What did that person do that was so helpful to you?
   - ❏ They encouraged me.
   - ❏ They taught me new concepts.
   - ❏ They affirmed my abilities.
   - ❏ They helped me discipline myself to develop my abilities.
   - ❏ They equipped me for what I was doing.
   - ❏ They believed in me.

"We know what we are, but know not what we may be."
—William Shakespeare

4. Below are some of the teachings of this passage which have a bearing on our reaching our potential. Using this scale (1= totally disagree to 10= totally agree), assign a number to each statement to indicate the degree to which you disagree or agree with them:

1	2	3	4	5	6	7	8	9	10
totally disagree				**somewhat agree**				**totally agree**	

   - ___ Women at times may exercise authority over men.
   - ___ Women in leadership is not acceptable in the modern church.
   - ___ Christ encouraged woman to be all that they can be.
   - ___ Paul encouraged woman to be all that they can be.
   - ___ It doesn't matter if we are men or women. The important thing is we identify our gifts and use them for Christ.
   - ___ We are all called to a life of service.
   - ___ Women can realize their potential in the church.

5. What type of role do you have in the church?
   - ❏ supportive
   - ❏ child care
   - ❏ administrative
   - ❏ mission
   - ❏ helping the needy
   - ❏ hospitality
   - ❏ teaching
   - ❏ leadership
   - ❏ music
   - ❏ other: _____

6. What role(s) would you like to have in your church?

- ❑ supportive
- ❑ child care
- ❑ administrative
- ❑ mission
- ❑ helping the needy
- ❑ hospitality
- ❑ teaching
- ❑ leadership
- ❑ music
- ❑ other: _____

LEADER: When you have completed the Bible Study, move on to the Caring Time (page 63).

7. What is keeping you from doing what you would like to do?

- ❑ my beliefs
- ❑ present church leaders
- ❑ the Bible
- ❑ my ignorance
- ❑ everything
- ❑ the belief of my family
- ❑ the beliefs of our church
- ❑ my fears
- ❑ nothing
- ❑ other: _____

8. If a "Priscilla" came along right now, what could she help you with in realizing your potential?

COMMENT

"Most people live physically, intellectually, or morally, in a restricted circle of their potential being. They make use of a very small portion of their consciousness and of their soul's resources, much like a man who uses only his little finger."
—William James

Priscilla was a Jewess who came out of Italy with her husband Aquila to live in Corinth. About a year and a half later they moved to Ephesus. Her prominence is evident by these factors. She became the teacher of the learned (and eloquent) Apollos. The church met in both her home in Rome, and later in Ephesus. She was widely known in the Christian world in her lifetime. Her husband and she "labored together." In spite of the general cultural position of women in the first century, Priscilla was mentioned first in four of the six references by Paul.

Priscilla and her husband were tentmakers. Their home was a meeting place for others who wanted to grow in their Christian faith. She was probably a studious woman with a good background in religion and Christianity. In Ephesus there was a well-organized congregation. And there Priscilla and Aquila ranked next to Paul and Timothy with their work in the congregation. It was in Ephesus that Priscilla and Aquila met Apollos and invited him into their home. There they expounded the Scriptures and taught Apollos the foundations of the Christian faith (1 Timothy 2:12). They were instrumental in the education of this later well-known Christian speaker and apologist.

Later, after the death of Claudius, Priscilla and Aquila returned to Rome. In writing Priscilla's name here for the last time, Paul used the diminutive Prisca. This reveals his intimate friendship with her.

CARING TIME / 15–45 Minutes / All Together

Leader: This is decision time. These four steps are designed to help you evaluate your group experience and to decide about the future.

EVALUATION

Take a few minutes to review your experience and reflect. Go around on each point and finish the sentences.

1. What are some specific things you have learned about realizing your potential?

2. Are you thinking or acting any differently because of your involvement in this study? In what way?

3. As I see it, our purpose and goal as a group was to:

4. We achieved our goal(s):
   - ❏ completely
   - ❏ somewhat
   - ❏ almost completely
   - ❏ We blew it.

5. The high point in this course for me has been:
   - ❏ the Scripture exercises.
   - ❏ discovering myself.
   - ❏ the fun of the fellowship.
   - ❏ the sharing.
   - ❏ belonging to a real community.
   - ❏ finding new life/purpose for my life.

6. One of the most significant things I learned was...

7. In my opinion, our group functioned:
   - ❏ smoothly, and we grew.
   - ❏ pretty well, but we didn't grow.
   - ❏ It was tough, but we grew.
   - ❏ It was tough, and we didn't grow.

8. The thing I appreciate most about the group as a whole is:

CONTINUATION

Do you want to continue as a group? If so, what do you need to improve? Finish the sentence:

"If I were to suggest one thing we could work on as a group, it would be ..."

MAKE A COVENANT

A covenant is a promise made to each other in the presence of God. Its purpose is to indicate your intention to make yourselves available to one another for the fulfillment of the purposes you share. In a spirit of prayer, work your way through the following sentences, trying to reach an agreement on each statement pertaining to your ongoing life together. Write out your covenant like a contract, stating your purpose, goals, and the ground rules for your group. Then ask everyone to sign.

1. The purpose of our group will be ... (finish the sentence)

2. Our goals will be ...

3. We will meet for _____weeks, after which we will decide if we wish to continue as a group.

4. We will meet from _____ to _____ and we will strive to start on time and end on time.

5. We will meet at _____ (place) or we will rotate from house to house.

6. We will agree to the following ground rules for our group (check):

   ❏ **Priority:** While you are in the course, you give the group meetings priority.

   ❏ **Participation:** Everyone participates and no one dominates.

   ❏ **Respect:** Everyone is given the right to their own opinion, and "dumb questions" are encouraged and respected.

   ❏ **Confidentiality:** Anything that is said in the meeting is never repeated outside the meeting.

   ❏ **Empty Chair:** The group stays open to new people at every meeting, as long as they understand the ground rules.

   ❏ **Support:** Permission is given to call upon each other in time of need at any time.

   ❏ **Accountability:** We agree to let the members of the group hold us accountable to the commitments which each of us make in whatever loving ways we decide upon.

CURRICULUM

If you decide to continue as a group for a few more weeks, what are you going to use for study and discipline? There are 15 other studies available at this 201 Series level. 301 Courses are for deeper Bible study, also with Study Notes.

For more information about small group resources and possible directions, please contact your small group coordinator or SERENDIPITY at 1-800-525-9563.